CHILDREN OF THE MISTS

Hugo McEwen

C

CENTURY
London Melbourne Auckland Johannesburg

For Mama and Papa

Copyright © Hugo McEwen 1987

First published in Great Britain in 1987 by
Century Hutchinson Ltd
Brookmount House, 62–65 Chandos Place
London WC2N 4NW

Century Hutchinson South Africa (Pty Ltd)
PO Box 337, Bergvlei, 2012 South Africa

Century Hutchinson Australia Pty Ltd
PO Box 496, 16–22 Church Street, Hawthorn
Victoria 3122, Australia

Century Hutchinson New Zealand Ltd
PO Box 40–086, Glenfield, Auckland 10
New Zealand

ISBN 0 7126 1686 1

Phototypeset by Input Typesetting Ltd, London SW19 8DR
Printed and bound in Great Britain by
WBC Bristol and Maesteg

Children of the Mists

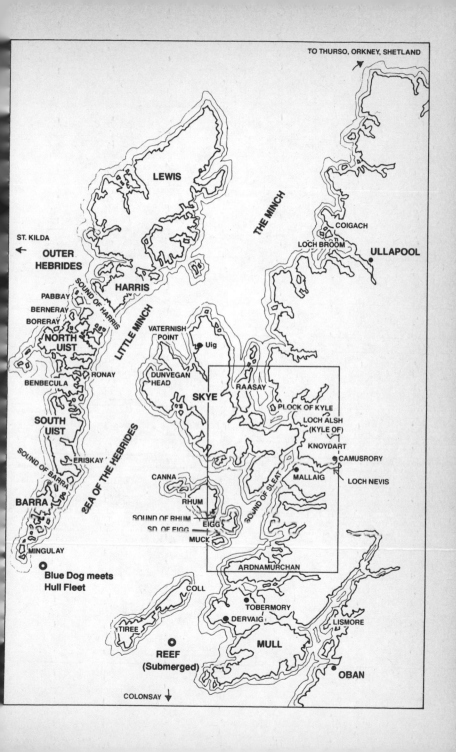

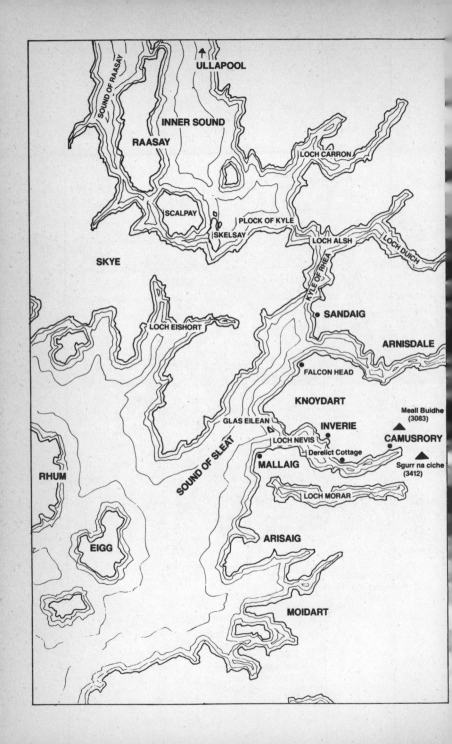

GLOSSARY

bide	stay
bothy	humble cottage or hut
cannae	can't
crofter	Highland smallholder
deid	dead
eejit	idiot
eleffen	eleven
Fenian	Catholic (Glasgow slang)
fitba	football
gey	very
ghillie	gamekeeper and guide
goan	going
heid	head
hiv tae	have to
ken	know
monarch	the largest, most regal stag, with the most points on its antlers, in any given area
morn's morn	tomorrow morning
no	not
nought	nothing

Old Firm match	Glasgow Rangers v. Celtic
polis	police
richt	right
sae	so
thon	that
werenae	weren't
wisnae	wasn't
yin	one

Prologue

The sun was setting, a heatless orange ball slipping into the white-flecked sea. It had been stormy; there was a curious hush, as if Nature were breathing a deep sigh of relief and steadying herself for the next onslaught. The huge, towering, laden clouds away to the north-west warned of worse to come; the Atlantic winter had more to hurl at the already battered cliffs of western Scotland. From the clifftops the sea looked deceptively calm, no longer – at least for the moment – the terrifying, thunderous turmoil that had spent its fury on the impassive cliffs shortly before. Now it rocked and surged, sucking away from the foot of the rock-strewn precipices and surging forwards again. Surge, suck, surge, suck. Calm . . . dangerously calm.

Up on the top of the cliff a young man squared his shoulders and ducked his head against the chill breeze. He squatted against a stunted, gnarled rowan bush and stared, emotionless, out to sea, occasionally moving his head to work out where the sun had reached. A peregrine falcon slid over the lip of the cliff and dipped down towards the water. The man moved slightly, turning his attention to the bird. There was a faint quack, a splash, and four eider duck lumbered clumsily into the air. The peregrine changed direction towards the flash of black and white, doubling his speed with two swift wingbeats. The eiders, no match for this, the quickest hunter they were ever likely

9

to meet, opted for their instinctive bolt-hole and flopped back on to the water. The peregrine swerved over them, letting out a shrill shriek, trying to scare them into further flight. But they had been lucky the first time and would not make the same mistake again. On the water they were safe from the predator, but in the air they were as good as dead.

The peregrine wheeled around and was back to the cliffs with a flap of his long, elegant wings. This time he was in luck. Momentarily befuddled as the falcon swept past, a rock dove dropped from its safe perch and clattered into a steep curve out to sea. The peregrine executed a perfect barrel roll and doubled back after the fleeing pigeon. Although it had a considerable start, the pursued had little chance of survival on its present course. In a straight line it was perhaps five miles to the colourless shore of Skye, to the west. The alternative was to double back into the teeth of the pursuer. For a minute it attempted the former. The watching man saw it recede to a black dot in the middle distance. But it did not have the speed or manoeuvrability to escape its hungry follower. Effortlessly the peregrine caught up and climbed high over the dove. The latter swerved, sensing danger, just as the falcon folded his wings against his flanks and swooped. Down he plummeted, with the speed of an arrow extending his talons at the last moment. Either the dove was very lucky, or it had perfect timing: with a split second to spare it banked sideways, turned and accelerated desperately back towards the mainland. Momentarily foiled, the peregrine soared out of his dive, looking around. He saw the dove and gave chase again, inches above the water. It is not for nothing that peregrines are known for their speed. He was flying now in earnest, immensely fast and unparalleled in aerobatics. He caught up with the pigeon yards short of the cliff.

Caught in the updraught rising off the precipitous wall both birds whipped over the young man. The falcon climbed over his prey, taking a passing lunge as it rose. The dove made a last desperate spurt, turning towards a sparse, low wood about a hundred yards inland. The peregrine was now high above, still climbing. He banked slightly and fell into a spiralling, corkscrew dive. The dove swerved wildly, covering the last hundred feet to the wood in seconds. But the peregrine was not going to be cheated. He altered direction in mid-dive and his great, lethal talons dropped. There was a puff of feathers as the two birds met. They crashed to the ground yards short of the wood.

The young man smiled slightly and stood up, rubbing his thighs. It was twilight now, darkening to an impenetrable, velvet black over his head. For a moment he turned away from the sea, then looked at his watch and turned back. Through the rising wind there was the vague splutter of an engine. The man looked around sharply, straining to catch the sound again. For a minute there was nothing but wind and sea. Then the sound came again, out to sea.

The last ray of the dying sun pierced the grey canopy and glittered dully across the water in a shaky path. The man produced a small pair of binoculars from his pocket and scanned the sea. He saw the flash of light catching on metal and focused the binoculars. Still as a statue he studied the boat in the twilit distance. A smile crept on to his face, a smile of triumph. He put the binoculars back into his pocket, and picked his way back up the hill.

The Pot of Gold

Two people were sitting in a small room. A coal fire glowed, throwing a warm light around the otherwise dark room. It was a sparsely furnished general bedroom-cum-sitting-room-cum-kitchen, with a bed in one corner, a stove in another, three heavy armchairs, a table and thick sheepskin carpets.

The girl sat slumped in an armchair, her head lolling backwards, her eyes lying closed so that the long, curving eyelashes pressed on her cheeks like the feet of tiny insects on the smooth surface of a pond. Her short, spiky blonde hair was dishevelled, as if her concept of brushing was to run her hands through it until it stood away from her ears and face. Even so a few strands fell over her forehead. Her face was thin and strong, with well-defined cheekbones, a narrow, straight nose and a mouth which never seemed to be fully closed. With a slight stretch of the imagination and somewhat more clothing than the simple white tee-shirt which barely covered what was obviously the body of a mature female, she could have been an effeminate boy in his late teens. With a little effort and perhaps a few touches of make-up she could have transformed herself into a very attractive young woman in her early twenties. As it was she was somewhere between the two. She was obviously exhausted, her breath coming in a heavy, heaving rhythm, rattling slightly somewhere in her throat. But she was not asleep; occasionally her eyes would flicker open, and her forehead would crease in a frown. The other person in the room was a middle-aged man. The rigours of the outdoor life he led gave the immediate impression of vigour and energy at the same time as ageing him beyond his years. His brown hair was beginning to grey at the temples; his face, although heavily lined, was healthy and full of strength. The result of years of squinting into the wind and rain was a permanent frown. Of all the lines on his leather-like face, those crossing his brow were the most deep, like tiny chasms running from one temple to the other.

Both looked as if they did not have an ounce of superfluous fat. When they moved, and even when they were still, their muscles were apparent, rippling and pushing against their clothes. The two of them, silently passing the time in the room, were peculiarly similar. The girl immediately gave the impression of incongruity, as if she belonged here only because she had forced herself, and the man was obviously someone who had seen many harsh winters, yet there seemed to be some affinity between them. They were like a young panther and an old lion who were dangerous in their own right, but who had agreed to put up with each other for their mutual advantage.

The man, hunched on the floor, his back to the fire, was bending his fingers on the floor, exerting enough weight on them to make them crack. One by one, with the ponderous method of someone who is acting mechanically whilst thinking about something completely different, he cracked the joints of his stubby fingers.

'I wish you wouldn't do that,' the girl said quietly, with a wince. He moved, stopping two fingers short of his left thumb. He looked up, expressionless. The girl yawned and arched her back.

'Isn't Jim back yet?' she asked through a second yawn.

13

'No.' The short negative left little chance for further elaboration or conversation. All the same the girl went on.

'Shouldn't we look for him?'

'He telt us tae bide.'

The girl glanced at her watch and stood up. For a moment she swayed dizzily and blinked. Then, regaining her equilibrium, she moved unsteadily to the fire and stretched her hands towards it.

'That was last night.'

'He'll come. He allus does.'

The girl walked to the only table in the room, a small kitchen stand with a wilted Formica top, littered with empty cigarette packets and bullets. A deer rifle, equipped with a telescopic sight, long magazine and silencer, leaned against the far wall, near the door. She picked up the rifle and deftly removed the magazine.

'Hud yer energy, woman,' the man remarked, eyeing her irritably. 'There'll be time enough fer running aboot in the morn's morn.'

At that moment the door opened beside her, letting in a blast of cold, salt-smelling wind. A young man entered, slammed the door shut with his foot, put a rifle beside its identical brother and kissed the girl. When he had broken away from the embrace he walked to the fire. He was around six feet tall, his thinness contributing to the impression of height. He was long-limbed, with the narrow, slender hands of an artist and long legs. His face was angular, bordering on gaunt with an aquiline nose and wide-set eyes which seemed to fluctuate between brown and green depending on the light. Now, in the dim glow of the fire they tended towards the latter. On seeing him for the first time it was a common reaction to think that he must have been a beautiful child. This was not to say that, without any doubt, he was a very handsome young man or that he had changed radically over the years. It

14

was simply that maturity had sharpened the angles on his face, giving it a harsh quality which would not have been there in his youth. His attraction was not so much aesthetic as wild. This was enhanced by his dishevelled appearance. His black hair was tangled and unkempt and his clothes were weatherbeaten and torn. For a while he stood in silence, with a vague smile, content to toast his back at the fluttering fire. The older man looked up, raising one eyebrow quizzically.

'Well,' he asked, 'get anything?'

The newcomer shrugged, his smile broadening to reveal a flash of uneven white teeth. 'Nothing we could eat or sell,' he replied in a voice which was languid to the point of being a drawl.

The girl, watching him with a mixture of love and amusement, exhaled a lungful of cigarette smoke in a laugh that was confined entirely to her nose. 'Not exactly the season for stalking, is it?'

The man glanced at her, his eyes smiling, then looked at his feet. 'Poaching knows no season,' he muttered. Then he moved his head slightly and caught the girl's eye. For a moment they stared at each other, as if a silent conversation were taking place. 'You were right, though,' he said quietly.

'What about?' she asked, creasing her brow.

'About the boat. I saw it this evening off Falcon Head.' A momentary look of triumph flickered across the girl's face. 'And you thought I was seeing things,' she replied.

He shrugged and moved his glance back to his feet. He was frowning. 'Well, it makes no sense, does it? There aren't any lobster pots out there and there are safer and better places and times to fish than under those cliffs on a January evening . . . It just doesn't make sense,' he concluded in a quiet, puzzled voice. The girl sat down heavily, shaking her head irritably as if to rid it of the

15

cobwebs which still lingered in her brain, fuddling her thoughts.

'I think,' she said at length, and then faltered, not sure of what she thought. ' . . . I don't get it either, but it could be . . .' She halted again and rubbed her eyes with the balls of her hands. It was a curiously childish gesture.

'Yes?' the boy prompted after a while.

'Well, I remember thinking at the time . . . or sort of wondering if they were . . . if they were sort of smuggling.' She looked up, smiling apologetically – just a silly thought that she should have kept to herself.

'Smuggling what?' the older man asked, speaking for the first time in some minutes. There was a look of disbelief in his eyes. But the mere fact that he had bothered to ask the question, instead of scorning it out of hand, gave her a little confidence.

'All sorts of things, like illegal immigrants, or stolen property out of the country, or . . .' Again she stopped, searching for further smugglable objects to back up her argument.

'Or drugs,' the boy put in simply. 'Now there's a thought,' he added, almost to himself, as if the idea appealed to him.

The older man looked from one to the other and a look of mild amusement softened his permanent frown. 'Well, there's nae harm in proving you fools,' he remarked. It was another way of admitting that he was interested too.

'No one fucks around in the Sound of Sleat for nothing at this time of year,' the boy said.

'Especially at night,' the girl added. By this time the older man was grinning, an unexpectedly mischievous smile on his hard, grim countenance.

'And there'll be a gale coming on,' he concluded, implying that no one in their right minds would not have noticed the warning signs in the sea and air, therefore no

16

one, presumably, was likely to risk being out at sea. The girl stood up and walked across to the boy. She draped her arms, straight with the hands hanging down, over his shoulders.

'What d'you think?' she mouthed. He smiled and slowly, deliberately nodded his head. The girl ran her tongue across her lower lip and turned her head to the other man, her eyebrows raised. He turned down the corners of his mouth and shrugged.

'Why no?' he remarked. His tone implied that he thought they were both being childish, but that he was willing to humour them. Both of the others knew that he was as inquisitive as they, but was unwilling to admit it. He had the natural right to be able to say 'Told you so' if they were disappointed, which came from age and command.

The small trawler moved out of Mallaig harbour. Ian MacGillavray, the seasoned fisherman who had taken The Honourable James MacGregor under his protective wing when James was no more than a wild teenager, and who had likewise adopted James's girlfriend Emma, had been ready to leave Mallaig for three days. When it had been decided, in the tiny house they used during the winter when they were poaching far out in the wilds, that they should show a more direct interest in the peculiar happenings out to sea, it was only a matter of hours before *Rob Roy* was chugging out for the same stretch of water, heaving across the surge.

Rob Roy was a small prawn-trawler, innocent-looking to any casual observer. But the fishermen of Mallaig and Oban loved her as much as they respected her owner. Ian MacGillavray was a legendary fisherman, who had been on the great whalers out of Peterhead as a child, and who knew every submerged rock, every reef, every shale and every current in the Western Isles like wayward but much-loved pets. Over the many years since he had come west, when the whaling died out, he had built up for his sturdy, manoeuvrable little boat a stockpile of equipment which was the envy of the Western Isles. He could, and frequently did, trawl in places so inaccessible and dangerous that the fact that they were illegal was irrelevant. No sane person would, or indeed could, follow him. The name *Rob Roy*, after the legendary Highland bandit-hero, was both an apt and a drily witty title for the most notorious poaching trawler in the Western Isles.

James MacGregor, Lord Assynt, had learnt about the sea from this man. After years of thankless, uphill toil he had not only many of the tricks and secrets that the western fishermen in general, and Ian MacGillavray in particular, had up their sleeves, but had also earned the friendship and respect of the xenophobic, grudging people he worked alongside. He was a brilliant navigator of the tricky archipelago which confuses the Atlantic coast of Scotland, and unparalleled as a poacher; so much so, in fact, that almost any seriously adventurous exploit of poaching anywhere inside a distance of one hundred miles of Oban was attributed to him, even if it was simply impossible that he could have done it.

'He wass in the pub wi' me an' Jock McReadie,' they would say, with mixed awe and pride; pride that they could say he had been with them (even when thirty other people in the pub could say the same).

'An' he ups an' leaves arooned eleffen, an' that' – a pause to give suitable weight to the punchline – 'that wass the nicht the pride o' Jura, a fifteen-pointer monarch, he wass that, wass poachit frae richt under thon head ghillie's nose.'

And whether it was true or not, James took the credit. It was a suitable arrangement with the other poachers – if it can be said that any grown man north of Lochgilphead

18

is not a poacher – who were willing enough to let MacGregor take the blame; he never got caught so why should he mind? But there was something in James that was more than just well-planned bravado: that was some of it, but not all. He had a quick, clever mind, sly and calculating. If MacGillavray could read the sea in a way that most people found uncanny, MacGregor could do the same with people. He knew what the police would do next before they did it, and made it his private occupation to make fools of them. This mixture of intuition, animal cunning, and childish playfulness, and a sort of wild, out-of-control *joie de vivre* made James a popular, if rarely seen, figure. But he himself had the common sense to know that all he was to these people was based on his friendship with Ian and the effect that this enigmatic old man had on him, even if the fishermen had forgotten this.

Emma Gaynor, by contrast, was the enigma in the eyes of the fisherfolk. Traditionally the place of women is to sit at home, keeping the fire burning and the broth hot, worrying themselves sick as they wait for their husbands and sons to return. But Emma had learned the ways of her lover quickly, and had demanded the right to join him on the trips he loved so much. She was a tough, wise girl, and knew that if she could never better the other contender to her man's heart then at least she could try to be on equal terms with it. After much acrimonious bickering, first with James and then between James and Ian, she was allowed to accompany them on one trip (on condition that she disguised herself as Jim's cousin, Robert MacGregor, so that at least no one else would know). And she had gone on the trip, eager to impress both men. On that first week Emma stalwartly overcame her initial nausea, an accomplishment in itself beyond many far stronger men, and she worked on overdrive to prove that she could do everything, and a little more, than was asked of her. Her sheer determination impressed Ian and Jim enough to make them forget their superstition, which said that a woman was bad luck as well as bad company on a trawler.

Although she made an unconvincing boy no one had yet thought to question her gender. It was unthinkable that any female should be seen near a boat, let alone working on one. Folk had accepted the cousin-of-Jim story, though the more lewd said that young Robert kept 'wee Jamie' or Ian, or perhaps both, warm on the cold nights of the fisherman. Either way, in two years no one particularly noticed, or indeed particularly cared what or who this unprepossessing effeminate young man was. Ian MacGilla-vray would not take someone on his boat unless he could do exactly what he ordered quickly, efficiently and without complaint. Not even a warm bed, as it were, would blind him enough to take a liability on board.

Therefore no one had looked twice as the three of them climbed on to *Rob Roy* yet again on this blustery Sunday night to go on escapades of fishing illegal waters, or poaching salmon and deer from the hundreds of million-aires' islands and estates dotted up the coastline. They had already accrued the notoriety of legends, and their deeds were spoken of with awe from Arran to Lewis. Being a legend had the dual effect of destroying one's privacy in some places whilst making it indestructible in others, and that was where their greatest secret lay. Because, whilst none of them could walk down a street in Oban or Mallaig without being noticed, Emma's secret held tight. If the people who surrounded them had taken the trouble to speak to, rather than about them, the secret could not possibly have remained intact. But who is a friend of a legend? Legends might be exposed to the public glare more than most people are, but they are very rarely known.

When they sailed from Mallaig harbour they went barely noticed. The occasional envious glance and admiring remark, and the muttered 'may you come back safe' from the old crone who sat on the harbour day and night, passing herself off as a witch and innocently joining into the air of superstition which seems to hang above the heads of sea-going folk the world over like black clouds.

When they had reached the open sea the waves began to kick the boat up and down. They did not notice the discomfort. Each one got on with his jobs unquestioningly. Ian steered straight out to sea, following the currents towards Mull until they were a safe distance from Mallaig. Then as dawn began to break, dull and unpleasant, he turned back into the Sound of Sleat and headed north, using the coast of Skye as a buttress against the worst of the elements.

Curtains of rain, drifting in from the north-west in grey swaths, obscured the mainland away to starboard. At first the drizzle on the window was light enough to disappear with one flick from the bridge-screen wiper. But it grew steadily worse. Waves coming from all directions in the treacherous currents began to throw *Rob Roy* into the air and then drop it into a trough with a sickening crash. When one broke directly over the bows it hurled tons of freezing sea water on to the boat, giving a similar effect to being thrashed by a gigantic wet towel.

The storm rose gradually to fever pitch as the day drew on. All three snatched their lunches – steaming coffee and hunks of brown bread – individually. In the late afternoon Ian gave up fighting the vicious cross-currents close to Skye and turned out into the sound. The full force of the storm hit them like a punch. In this part of the world a storm may blow up in minutes and die as unexpectedly. But that ability, designed by Nature to catch out any fool who does not know what he's doing, does not in any way detract from the power of these storms as they rage. They are Nature at her most cruel and violent. Both Jim and Emma were drenched as they made brief forays from the cabin, to pick up loose creels and ropes and to unblock the scuppers vital for draining the waterlogged deck. Each time they returned to the cabin, their oilskins dripping, their hair lank with salt-laden spray and rain, their bodies shivering uncontrollably.

All day Ian had limited his conversation to the barest necessities, curtly ordering the others to do this or that and immediately sinking back into the silence of concentration which accompanied his job. But as the short winter twilight drew in he became nervous and agitated.

'Where d'you see them from, Jim?' he asked worriedly.

'Falcon Head . . . up in Knoydart.' Ian laughed drily at this.

'You'll get yersel caught up there, yin o' these days. Ye hivnae stopped poaching it in six months.'

'It's fair game,' Jim replied with a shrug. 'I've been up there . . . what, thirty times? . . . yeah, 'bout that, in the last three months, and I haven't once seen one ghillie or crofter. Besides,' he grinned at Ian's back, 'I don't poach . . . I share.'

'Wi' who?' Ian asked with a snort.

'You, Emma.'

'Right wee socialist, you.'

'I use the gifts God gave me as best I can,' Jim replied in a deliberately pompous voice.

Emma, who was watching the conversation with a cigarette hanging out of her mouth and a broad grin on her face, giggled. 'I like the idea of using God's gifts to break the law,' she remarked.

Jim turned to her, smiling. 'Whose side're you on?'

'The one who looks most like winning,' she replied, still grinning.

'Fickle bitch,' he answered.

And so on. Always, in times when the stress of living so

22

close to each other in pretty cramped conditions looked like becoming too great, a sure way of dispersing some of the aggression was to have one of these insult-flinging, bickering playfights. No one thought much about them and what had been said was soon forgotten, but they almost invariably succeeded in clearing the air – although the language flung around was occasionally so expressively foul that they even succeeded in shocking each other.

The talking had long since died out, giving way to a silence devoted to private reveries, when Ian cut into Loch Hourn and rounded the north-west corner of Knoydart. The wind had risen to a screaming crescendo and the rain was now driving sleet. It was pitch dark outside the cabin. Ian switched on the powerful spotlights that Emma, who had suddenly found in herself a knack for mechanics which both surprised and delighted her partners, had installed on the roof of the cabin. Most of the light they were now casting was reflecting on the billions of water particles in the air.

'I cannae see the focking coast, Jim,' Ian remarked quietly. 'Ye'll hiv tae go out an' turn yin o' they spotlights.' Jim nodded and donned a lifejacket. He pulled his oilskin over the top and disappeared out on to the deck. A moment later he appeared again, hugging the side of the cabin as he edged his way along the runner-board to the front of the boat. After some fiddling with a spanner he adjusted the light, swinging it around towards the cliffs, and tightened the bolt again. He then climbed back along the side. Emma, who was watching him intently through the spray-covered windows, saw him stop about halfway and squint astern. The wind whipped his hair across his face and he tossed it back, mouthing an oath. He glanced at his feet, to check that they were in the right place, safely on the narrow runner-board, and hurried the rest of the way. He pushed into the cabin and slammed the door shut.

'What's up?' Emma asked.

'Think we've got company,' he said, still breathing heavily.

'It's no Arnisdale?' Ian asked. Jim shook his head, biting his lip.

'Arnisdale's ten miles back, at least. You'd be lucky if you saw two hundred yards in this weather.'

'Mebbe . . .' Ian remarked uncertainly. 'Here, take the wheel. I'll go and look.' He gave the wheel to Jim and crossed the cabin. He pressed his face against the glass and stared out into the darkness. Emma came beside him and did the same.

'You're richt enough, though. There's a big boat and it's no more than half a mile behind us.'

'And it sure as hell isn't the police at this time of night,' Emma added.

'It's weird,' Ian concluded quietly.

Jim, working completely from memory and guesswork, found Falcon Head and they slowed down, turning this way and that, looking for a buoy or some other marker. It took tantalizingly long to find what he was looking for, but at last his lights caught on a shiny object ahead. It was a dark-blue buoy, suspicious in itself because dark blue is not a colour one would choose to contrast with the sea. This buoy, it seemed, was not meant to be seen. Jim gave the wheel back to Ian and accompanied Emma on to the deck. They drew up beside the small, bobbing object and Jim flicked on a torch as Ian turned off every other light on the boat. For a moment the boat swayed violently, then steadied. Jim gave the torch to Emma and picked up a boat-hook whilst Emma watched nervously as the boat behind closed in. Four separate lights, in a square, could be discerned. She could see the cabin light, large and wide, in the middle of the square. It was the cabin of a cruiser, the sort that the millionaires owned. Jim was now sitting

24

astride the side of the boat with the boat-hook stretched out into the darkness.

'Can you see it?' Emma yelled above the gale.

'Closer. I need a foot closer.' His words wafted over. Emma glanced at the oncoming boat and then passed the order to Ian. *Rob Roy* edged closer to the cliffs, now only seventy or eighty feet away. The surge, as the waves rebounded off the cliff and fell back on each other, bucked and heaved the trawler. The noise of the wind, the waves crashing over *Rob Roy* and the defeaning explosions of sound as the sea unleashed its full fury on the already battered mainland, made everything else inaudible. Therefore Emma was surprised and suddenly frantically scared when she glanced again at the following boat and was blinded as the full glare of the spotlights fell on her. She squinted, raising a hand to shade her eyes.

'Quickly, Jim! He's on top of us,' she shouted desperately. Jim did not turn to see this for himself. He steadied himself, drawing on almost superhuman reserves of self-control to calm his nerves. He leant out and made a last, wild thrust for the small blue buoy which bobbed inches out of reach. The boat-hook caught on the rope which attached the buoy to whatever hung underneath. He dragged in the pole, hand over hand, and grabbed the cold, slippery rope. The cruiser was slowing up as it drew in behind. Jim turned to the cabin, even as he hauled on the rope.

'Get the fuck out of here!' His voice rose even above the storm. *Rob Roy* lurched forwards while Jim held on to the cord for dear life. As the trawler gathered speed, and whatever was tied to the buoy began to drag, resisting the speed at which it was forced to travel through the water, the rope pulled through his hands, tearing the skin from his palms. At the same moment there was a crack from behind, and something thudded into the wood at Emma's

25

feet. She leapt like a scorched cat and swore viciously. Almost immediately a similar crack followed, and the glass of the cabin door exploded inwards.

'They're shooting at us, the bastards!' Emma yelled in disbelief and anger. Ian could be heard shouting obscenities from the cabin. He swung the boat around and *Rob Roy*, shaking violently from the pressure suddenly exerted on its small engine, veered out to sea and away from the deadly path of the spotlights. The pursuers turned immediately and a few more shots could be heard through the turmoil; they went wide, sliding silently into the mountainous sea.

Ian came out of the cabin and joined Jim at the rope.

'Go steer,' he ordered, looking at Emma. Amazed at the request she looked over her shoulder, thinking that he was talking to someone else. Never before had Ian allowed her anywhere near the controls.

'Go on,' Jim snapped. Without further thought she obeyed and ran into the cabin. Whatever was on the end of the rope seemed to weigh a ton. Hand over hand, foot by foot, Jim and Ian strained until the muscles from their shoulderblades to the tips of their fingers were screaming for release. At last they gained enough excess rope to attach it to the winch meant for hauling in the nets. With a last, supreme effort they threw themselves backwards. Something large and metallic leaped over the side on to the deck. For a moment, a split, bemused second, Jim found himself thinking that it looked like a tuck box he used to have when he was at prep school. It was rectangular, about a foot wide, two feet long and a foot deep. It seemed, at first glance, to be one unbroken metal object, without lock, key or lid. But on closer inspection it did have a join, about three inches from the top, which was expertly welded together. Whatever it contained, it was not designed to be broken into, either by inquisitive humans or by the sea.

But there was little time for closer inspection. The bullets began to whistle overhead again, a few hitting the boat, most missing. Emma pulled out the throttle all the way and threw all of her ten stone to starboard, dragging the wheel around as she plunged on to the deck. The boat swerved northwards, into the fury of the storm. Gigantic waves broke over the prow as *Rob Roy* cut through them, landing on the small craft with sickening thumps. The two men were hurled to the planks like a pair of matchsticks. For a moment the weight of the water pinned them down. Then Jim grabbed a knife from his belt and crawled to the box. Ian threw himself into the cabin as another bullet embedded itself in the wood a handspan from his left ear. Jim kept his head low and worked on the thick rope with renewed ferocity. At last he succeeded in severing it by stretching it on the deck and hacking away with short, powerful strokes. The moment it parted he grabbed the heavy box and ducked into the cabin. Ian, who was back at the wheel, spun *Rob Roy* around and cut straight back in towards the cliffs. The spotlights lost them momentarily and swung wildly around before picking them up again. Ian, who was watching the four pinpoints of light in the reflection on the glass in front of him, hurled *Rob Roy* back out to sea. He grimaced.

'She's no liking the speed, though,' he remarked quietly.

'Will she make it to Mallaig?' Emma asked worriedly. Ian shrugged, his back still turned.

'Mebbe, mebbe no . . . I'm no heading for Mallaig anyways.' Jim looked up sharply. He had been nursing his torn palms until then, but this cut off his self-pity in midstream.

'What d'you mean?' he asked. Ian glanced over his shoulder and let out a short, fierce laugh.

'I'm going for Knoydart.'

At this both Jim and Emma laughed in disbelief. Knoydart is a large bay which comes to a narrow mouth, the only opening on to the open sea. The currents and the narrowness of the mouth are hard to navigate even on a calm, clear day.

'Without lights? You have to be kidding.' It was Jim who at last broke the amazed silence.

'A'hm serious.'

'That's crazy.'

'Aye.'

'It's not possible.'

'Aye, it is.'

'Have you ever done it?'

'Allus a first time.'

Jim thought about this for a moment, then ran his tongue over his lips, tasting salt on the cracked skin.

'Is it possible?' he asked quietly.

'Aye . . . with a wee bitty luck.'

He turned the boat out to sea for the last time and the shoreline, which had been cutting away to port, barely visible in the darkness, disappeared again astern. Jim picked up the one rifle they had taken and slowly, almost dreamily, clipped on the full magazine and slammed the bolt back and then forward again, slipping one of the lethal, pointed shells into the breach.

Whoever was following was determined not to lose their prey. They swerved out to sea and then thought better of it and cut back in to port, obviously trying to cut off *Rob Roy* from Mallaig, which lay ten miles away to the south-west. Ian slowed slightly, allowing his adversary to come up aside, about fifty yards away. Jim rested the gun on the broken window and hunched down, staring into the sight.

'Don't kill anyone,' Emma said with a dry smile. Jim's voice came back, muffled against his outstretched left arm.

'I'm not aiming for people.'

Two of the spotlights shone against the side of the trawler

28

and bullets began to thud into the wood. The sea was heaving, making accurate shooting on both sides almost impossible. Jim waited for two or three long minutes. At one point he laughed. 'It's like the bloody Golden Shot.'

At last he seemed to be ready. He took two deep breaths and slowly squeezed the trigger. Emma and Ian, who were watching eagerly, saw the red flash from the barrel a split second before the report. The butt kicked Jim's shoulder back. One of the spotlights simultaneously went dark, and Jim turned and loosed off the remaining four shots. The first two were perfect, knocking out the powerful spotlights with stunning accuracy. The last two shots, however, missed their final mark. But it was a superb sequence of shots, so incredible, in fact, that neither Ian nor Emma could speak for some seconds. Then Ian's wrinkled, nut-brown face broke into a broad grin.

'Fock me,' he remarked admiringly. Emma walked across as Jim laid the rifle carefully on the floor and draped herself over him, kissing him long and hard on the lips.

'That was bloody unbelievable,' she said at last, breaking away. Jim shrugged modestly.

'No sae bad,' he replied.

Ian was quick to use the advantage Jim had won. With only one light left, the other boat would not be able to see something ten yards away whereas Ian could see for quite a distance. He turned the boat almost back on itself and hammered every last bit of throttle into the small engine. *Rob Roy* lurched forwards, turning in an arc around the stern of the cruiser, not more than fifteen feet away from it. As they swung past, Emma pressed her face to the side of the cabin and stared intently at the cruiser.

'It's registered at Oban,' she said. 'It's called . . . *Argos*, I think. Yes, *Argos*.' She turned to Jim. 'Ever heard of it?'

'Nope. But only some pretentious, rich git would call a cabin cruiser *Argos*.'

'Shouldnae be too difficult tae check up on it,' Ian remarked.

By now they were well clear of the cruiser. For the first time in the chase the predators had lost touch. Ian stalled the engine and allowed the boat to be driven in towards the coast. As he was still running without any guiding lights, turning into Knoydart was a matter of supreme judgement and a great deal of good luck. Even if they had still been using their spotlights they would not have seen the strait until they were into it. Without realizing it, they were driven through the narrow mouth and into the bay. Suddenly everything became calm. The full force of the gale was completely shut off by the surrounding hills; the water was choppy but no longer in the least dangerous. Lights twinkled away across the bay. Ian turned on the engine again and steered the boat to port, where the promontory which rose, steep and crowned with trees, on the northern side of the mouth, cut back into a sheltered little bay. He turned off the engine and wiped beads of sweat from his forehead with the back of one hand.

'We did it,' he said, with the vaguest hint of triumph in his voice. Jim stared out towards the lights of Inverie, across the bay. He looked over his shoulder at Ian, a smile lighting up his face like the sun appearing from behind a cloud.

'You did it,' he said quietly. Emma let out a whoop of joy and dived into Ian's arms, planting a smacking kiss on his lips.

'You did it, you old bugger! You fucking well did it!' she yelled, prancing back across the cabin, skipping with joy. Ian grinned sheepishly and sat down.

'Even I thought thon wisnae possible,' he said, his voice gruff.

After a few minutes of waiting to see whether anyone else came into the bay, Jim turned on the engine.

'Where to?' he inquired. Ian looked up tiredly.

'They lights yonder. Thon's Inverie. We'll lie up there fer the nicht.'

Half an hour later all three sat around a small table in the only pub on Knoydart, one of the thirty-odd houses which made up the village of Inverie. There were six pints of heavy on the table, six double whiskies and two packets of cigarettes. This was not so much a celebration as an attempt to calm their jarred nerves. Even before they had landed on the jetty the enormity of what had happened out to sea began to dawn on them. Someone had chased them for four hours, across forty miles of sea in an appalling storm, and had made several attempts on their lives. However serious and earnest their previous escapades had been, they had been games compared to this. This was for real.

'Well, if it was the police I'm writing to my MP.' Emma's voice betrayed her. Beneath the brave, dry joke was more than a hint of hysteria.

Ian did not smile. He looked at his beer, expressionless. 'They werenae aiming tae miss, were they?' he remarked simply.

This reduced them to a pensive silence again. When they had disembarked, the boat had looked like one of those fighter aeroplanes which always seem to limp home just as the petrol gives out, in war comics: all bullet holes and shattered glass. Emma had said, with fearful wonder, that it looked like a colander; and then had run up to the pub, suddenly in bad need of a stiff drink.

After a couple of hours they all returned to *Rob Roy* in a maudlin condition, and slept on the boat. Ian and Emma were too exhausted to stay awake for more than a minute

31

after they had hit their beds. But Jim tossed and turned restlessly for seven hours, longing for just an hour of sleep but being denied even that. In the end he gave up the fight and quietly got out of his bunk. He pulled on a tee-shirt and a pair of jeans, and climbed up into the cabin. Away to the east, behind the ragged mountains of Argyll, the sun shed a dull red glow on the smattering of high herringbone clouds. The snow-capped mountains glistened in the half-light before dawn. The storm had blown itself out and the silence was like a noise in itself, pressing into Jim's ears. Somewhere, away up in the trees to the left, a crow cawed raucously and Jim briefly wondered why it was always the crows who woke first. Then came the blackbirds and the sparrows. But the crows were always just a bit before.

'Bet *they* aren't after worms,' he thought aloud, realizing what a fatuous, ridiculous proverb that particular one was.

'S'pose they're all pretty idiotic,' he said aloud again, more to hear his own voice than because he was genuinely interested in this peculiar train of thought. He smiled to himself and put a kettle on to boil. He lit a cigarette and drew heavily, exhaling a stream of small, perfect smoke rings, which wafted across the still cabin, growing to the size of footballs before they broke up and dispersed. The kettle came to the boil and Jim made himself a cup of coffee, humming almost inaudibly. He sat down with his coffee and stared out of the window. As the sun came up over the mountains – a big orange ball which had as little power as the moon or the stars to thaw the frost-whitened fields which hugged the shoreline – slowly, steadily, light caught on something to Jim's left and the dull gleam caught his eye. He turned and suddenly remembered the box. It looked smaller now than it had. An iron container, somewhat dirtied by seaweed and salt, but solid.

Jim stared at it for some time. It had no latch or keyhole, and there seemed to be no way of opening it other than brute force. After a bit of perfunctory feeling around, prising and pulling, he realized that it was going to be more trouble than he had originally thought. He picked it up, noticing again with surprise how heavy it was, and carried it out on to the deck.

From a cupboard in the cabin he produced a heavy screwdriver and a big hammer like a mini sledgehammer. He put the point of the screwdriver to the join and carefully, then less carefully, then downright violently hammered away. Whoever had welded it together did not intend opening it to be easy. It took Jim over an hour to make a hole that was big enough for a crowbar to fit into. He then put a very heavy box on top of the metal case and jumped on to the crowbar. The very heavy box leapt into the air and landed with a crash on its side. Unperturbed, Jim hunted out a second crowbar and succeeded in forcing it in alongside the first. He then braced himself, rubbed his hands, and heaved them in opposite directions, using his body as the fulcrum and the equally distributed force as a pivot to push the lid off. After two failed attempts he succeeded. The crack widened visibly, there was a sharp snap and the two halves parted company. The contents landed on the deck with a dull thud.

'Jesus!' Jim's eyes almost started from his head when he saw what lay before him. There were about thirty square bags, each about two pounds in weight, every one filled with white powder. For a moment he stared, agape.

'Sure as hell isn't sugar,' he muttered. Then, suddenly nervous, he looked around to make sure that no one had seen, scooped the bags into one of the discarded halves of the box and rushed into the cabin. Downstairs someone was moving around. Jim put his head to the hatch and called down the stairs, fighting to keep his voice calm.

'Emma?'

'Yeah?'

'Could you come up here a sec?'

'Sure.'

She climbed up the stairs to the cabin and hopped on to the floor.

'I'm feeling much bet . . .' The word was never finished. Her eyes had lit on the white bags and were wide open with surprize. She glided across the floor, feeling herself in a dream, and picked up one of the bags. Taking a sheath knife from her belt she slit the bag, poked her forefinger in and tasted the white dust. She rolled her eyes.

'Cocaine,' she remarked simply.

'You sure?'

'Sure I'm sure. I used to be hooked on the stuff.'

'You never told me that.' Jim sounded hurt.

Emma looked at him and answered with a quick smile. 'You never asked.'

'That's worth quite a bit, yes?' Jim asked tentatively. Emma eyed him with the faintest smile.

'Quite a lot? . . . Yes it is. And Mount St Helen's was quite a bonfire.'

'How much?'

This time Emma could not contain her joy. A huge, beaming grin suffused her tired face.

'Millions. That's gold dust. There must be fifty pounds of it at least . . . I should say that almost nothing on earth is worth as much, per ounce, as this.'

At that moment Ian appeared through the hatch and saw the pile of laden bags. He rubbed his eyes and yawned. 'That's drugs,' he said slowly, 'or my dick's a kipper.'

Jim smiled and replied slowly, 'The reputation of your dick's safe. It's cocaine.'

He dragged the last word dreamily, as if he both enjoyed and mistrusted the taste it left in his mouth.

Ian nodded sagely and surprised his two young companions by sitting down heavily, saying, 'Aye, it would be . . . we really stuck our heids in the wasps' nest this time.' He shook his head and glowered at the cocaine with a look of utter distaste. After a while he shook his head again. 'Tell you a story about thon stuff,' he said quietly, deliberately. 'A guy . . . name of Jack Hardon, found some o' thon on the beach down Oban way. "Oho," thinks he, "aff tae Glesgae and flog this here dope. It'll make us enough money tae settle doon wi' the video an' a microwave an' lots o' kids . . . " – guid Fenian wis Jack. So aff he drives, the boot o' his car stuffed wi' all it could hold. An' he gets tae Glesgae and makes a few inquiries. But the moment he mentions it, he has half the polis in Strathclyde aifter him, as well as all the big drug boys, doon on him like a ton o' bricks. A week later the polis found him – in a gutter in Paisley wi' his heid all staved in.'

This put a dampener on the general euphoria. Jim stared at the offending articles and sat down opposite Ian, lighting a cigarette. 'So what d'you suggest?' he asked.

'Lie low,' came the immediate answer. 'They werenae hiving a laugh last nicht, an' *Rob Roy*'s no sae difficult tae identify.'

Emma sat down on the third chair and gloom descended on the small group. The only movements for some minutes were the clouds of smoke issuing in blue-grey swirls and rings from the mouths of Emma and Jim. Ian took a cigarette from Emma's packet and lit a match. He shielded the flame elaborately in cupped hands and dragged hard on the cigarette, as if some non-existent gust of wind was about to blow out the flame, and great care as well as speed was needed to combat this; a habit common to many people used to smoking outside. After a few moments Jim stirred and flicked ash on to the floor.

'I never knew you smoked,' he remarked.

'I gave up,' Ian answered, the cigarette hanging out of the corner of his mouth.

35

Emma looked up, raising her eyebrows. 'What does it taste like?' she asked irrelevantly.

'Like it smells,' Ian replied. He rolled his eyes and smiled. 'Dee-li-shus,' he added, enunciating every syllable as if they were different words.

Emma laughed quickly. Suddenly it seemed that the gloom had dispersed just as the smoke dispersed around the cabin. One question and one short answer, a few infinitely precious words, had the power to beat back all the negative emotions, hanging like vultures over a dying animal.

'I s'pose,' Jim began uncertainly, 'there can't be too many cruisers called *Argos* up here. It wouldn't be difficult to trace it.'

'And meanwhile?' Emma asked, dropping her cigarette and grinding it to death with the heel of her gym shoe.

'Meanwhile, we hide the coke, the boat and ourselves,' Jim replied, adding in the same tone of voice, 'and refrain from making such a godawful mess on the clean floor.'

Emma looked up, vague surprise registering in her eyes. 'Fucking hyprocrite.'

Blue Dog

After some debate it was agreed that they would hide out in a bothy at the furthest end of Loch Nevis, the loch that cut like a huge fist, one finger pointing eastwards, into the huge Knoydart estate. It was a bungalow called Camus-rory, built with wood and corrugated iron, used for Outward Bound courses in summer time, but empty for the rest of the year.

Loch Nevis is in fact two lochs: the main one is the larger, comprising, to pursue the metaphor, the fist. This was the one into which Ian had so skilfully navigated his way on the previous evening, at the end of the chase. From the mouth, which opens on to the Sound of Sleat, to Inverie it is no more than two miles as the cormorant flies, or as the trawler chugs. But southwards the loch opens out and stretches for another six or seven miles of barren, unpopulated coastline. The southernmost tip of the loch is almost opposite Mallaig, but separated by miles of harsh, unfriendly hills. At the south-west corner there are a few houses and a church. East of that the loch narrows to a second mouth, only a couple of hundred yards across. Beyond this is an inner loch, unguessed at unless one knows of its existence beforehand. It is long and narrow, about half a mile across at its widest, and just over two miles long. At the furthest end of this, tucked away amongst the

37

trees and hills, with its own jetty, stands the bothy where they had decided to stay.

The morning after the chase they bought as many provisions as the tiny village shop in Inverie could spare. These were meagre and unsatisfactory, as Inverie had the dubious honour of being almost entirely cut off from the outside world during the winter. It was reached by a small trawler from Mallaig once a week, which carried little more than the barest necessities: perishables, like bread, butter and, ironically, fish; and the essentials, namely whisky and beer. Other than that, the little community was completely self-sufficient.

Having bought what they could, they set off down the loch, stopping on the way to inform the people who lived at the southern end what they were doing. They seemed unperturbed. As far as it went, there was nothing new in fishermen or poachers hiding out at times of crisis: in particular, times when the local polis were too close behind for comfort, and time was needed to slink away while the trouble died down. And the people of the west coast and Western Isles are an easygoing, undemanding lot; they ask no questions and except only a perfunctory explanation, accepting truth and lies with the same bored resignation. Stopping to talk to them was a gesture, but a well-judged one. They knew *Rob Roy* and all who sailed in it. They would guard Ian's, Jim's and 'Bob's' privacy as jealously as they guarded their own.

Ian dropped Jim and Emma at the bothy, and emptied the boat of the provisions and all the traces of their 'catch' of the previous evening. He left almost immediately to collect more provisions, some more weapons and ammunition, and some information from Mallaig. Jim kept the only rifle. He toyed with it, turning it over and caressing it gently with one forefinger. With this friend and support to bolster up his courage and virility, he felt considerably safer.

The moment *Rob Roy* disappeared up the loch, Ian's crew metamorphosed into lovers. They ran up the stairs into the bothy and entered, ignoring the pile of provisions in the hall. Jim lit a fire in what must have been a common room for the Outward Bounders when they relaxed, exhausted, at the end of each long day. Emma undressed. It was by now well after midday, and already the day was drawing to its conclusion. The sky had returned to its interminable hue of watery grey. The sun was beginning to contemplate laying down its head for the night somewhere between the wild, empty mountains and infinity. Already the bothy was cast into shadow by the squatting bulks of the mountains, which crouched in close to the shore like huge neolithic men, huddled up against the cold. Jim undressed slowly in front of the fire, feeling goose pimples rise on his legs and arms. He looked at Emma and saw a pretty, well-proportioned girl standing like a marble statue before him: no longer his invented cousin, but his fiancée and lover of four years. They came together gently and kissed for a long time in front of the fire. There was a languid patience in their passion: not the wild, uncontrollable frenzy of adolescent love, but the quiet, calm relaxation of infinitely more mature lovers. Their relationship, in fact, was more mature than many affairs of far longer standing. They were first and foremost great friends.

They broke away at last, breathing gasps of minuscule ice particles at each other. A smile crept on to Jim's face.

'Now tell me,' he muttered, 'or for ever hold my piece . . .' Emma laughed, baring her white teeth and throwing back her head. She traced a line with her forefinger across Jim's cheek.

'What do you want to know, wicked bastard?'

'Have you been screwed by Ian?'

'. . . If I said yes?' she whispered.

'I might kill you,' Jim replied, equally quietly.

'You might not, though.'

'True enough.'

'So what's the alternative?' Jim smiled and planted a quick kiss on her lips. 'I might ask how many times!'

Emma laughed. She put her hands on his shoulders and pulled him down to the carpet.

Half an hour later they lay naked in each other's arms, with the red glow of the fire playing on their bodies, an elaborate masterpiece of hide and seek between light and shadow on their lithe frames. Emma's eyes were closed and she was breathing in shallow, irregular gasps. Jim shook her slightly and her eyes fluttered open, for a second childish and vulnerable. Then, when she realized where and with whom she was, the look was replaced by an affectionate, questioning gaze.

'What is it?' she murmured.

'You still haven't answered my question,' Jim replied in an almost inaudibly low mutter.

'If I tell you, will you let me go to sleep? I'm so comfortable.'

'I promise,' Jim answered. There was a brief pause.

'Twice,' Emma remarked simply.

'Was he good in bed?'

'Rough.'

'Serves you right.' They fell alseep again.

When Emma awoke it was with the nagging feeling that something was not as it should have been. There was a noise, intertwined with her dream, that should not have been there. She surfaced into wakefulness, vaguely confused. Then, as her conscious mind clawed its way to the fore, it clicked into place suddenly that what she had heard was a voice. Startled, she shook Jim, a little more violently than she should have. He woke with a start, letting out a little cry, then relaxed in her arms.

'What is it? It's still night-time.'

'People, I think. Down on the jetty,' she whispered.

It was amazing how quickly Jim awoke. He was on his feet before she finished the sentence and across to the window in a flash. He peered through the window and ducked back across the room, grabbing his trousers. Emma was already half-dressed. They were fully clad in a matter of seconds. Jim grabbed the rifle, thrust two boxes of shells into his pockets, and ran to the far door. Emma, meanwhile, scooped up the bags of cocaine – now in a potato sack from *Rob Roy* – and ran across to Jim.

'Out the back door,' he ordered in a hoarse whisper.

They slunk out of the house and closed the door gently behind them.

'Get across the garden and up that hill,' he said, gesticulating to where the steep slope rose like a huge, empty blackness in the off-black night sky. 'I'm going to take a look,' he added.

He slipped around the corner of the bungalow before she could argue. For a moment she swayed, torn between her urge to follow Jim and her knowledge that she should obey him. Then she turned and sprinted across the field which passed for a garden, leapt over the low dyke and waded into the heather. Three years of staying upright on heaving decks, or stalking across the moors on one of her frequent deer-poaching expeditions either with Jim or, of late, on her own, had toughened Emma. The girl who had been a wild teenager in London and had left, aged eighteen to go on a holiday with her boyfriend in Scotland, had all but gone. The holiday, with occasional sub-holidays, had lasted three years now and did not seem in immediate danger of ending.

She had returned home to her family in Essex twice. Both

41

times just succeeded in worsening her truncated, almost terminally ill, relations with the other members of her family. She had argued constantly with her father, a retired naval commander, who saw Jim as a wild, dangerous half-gypsy (which was true enough, as his mother was Yugosla-vian), and his daughter as a fool, and a bewitched fool at that. Her mother had cried constantly; her two brothers had stayed clear, not wishing to aggravate their father nor lose the love of their sister. And she had called them 'gutless, spineless wimps' for their pains. All in all, the ensuing ritual of disinheritance which her father went through to try scaring her back into the fold turned out to be a formality. She had deliberately and consciously spurned any small inheritance she had coming to her. Jim and Ardellan, his pretty little castle between Mallaig and Arisaig, were her inheritance.

When she had left London she could not have run half the length of the King's Road without ending up in some shop or bar, her breath coming in creaky rasps. Now she could run to the top of this steep slope without undue discomfort. Aching calves, a stop to shift her sixty-pound load and another stop to look back for Jim, hoping that he would catch up, were the only irregularities. Jim did not catch up just then. She saw the lights of the bothy flicking on as people searched from room to room. Then the back door burst open, throwing an arc of light across the garden. The beams of torches poked up the hillside, and there was the report of a gun going off. Emma hesitated momentarily, then turned and struck out up the hill again.

After half an hour she was on the summit of the hill. She sat down in the damp heather and glanced at her watch for the first time since she had woken up. It was twenty to three: another four and a half hours, at least, until dawn. During her climb she had thought that she felt spots of fine drizzle on her face. She had dismissed this from her mind by convincing herself that they were tiny beads of sweat. But now, as she sat still up on the hill, she found that actually a light, cold rain was falling. As she was contemplating this misfortune Jim came loping over the brow of the hill.

'They're following us. There's about ten of them,' he succeeded in gasping out. 'And it's bloody snowing.'

'Snowing?' Suddenly it struck Emma that such a soft, cold drizzle was unlikely to be anything else at this time of year. 'Oh shit.' She stood up and hitched her burden into as comfortable a position as possible.

'I'll carry that if you want,' Jim offered unenthusiastically.

'And leave me to shoot at people?'

'I was rather hoping we wouldn't have to.'

'It's a chance I'd prefer not to take, if it's okay by you.' Jim snorted mirthlessly. 'Fine by me.'

'Okay, let's be off then.' They both took a few deep breaths, stretched their legs, and began to jog away across the hill.

Together they ran through the dark, cold night. They had a choice: either they could make for Inverie over Meall Buidhe, which was something over three thousand feet at its highest. This route meant that they would take at least until dawn, and would spend the coldest part of an already cold night on an exposed, high hill. The alternative was to find a nice, secluded peat hag and risk exposure by lying in that until dawn came. Meanwhile they had to shake off their pursuers. They ran up and down the peaty hills, jumped over streams and waded, knee-deep, through clammy, malodorous bogs.

At last, after an age of running, they ground to a halt, exhausted and lost. The snow was congealing before it fell, drifting around, weightless and fluffy, speckling the night sky. It takes a walk on a cold night in the middle of nowhere to see snow as something a little more sinister than a pleasant substance designed for the amusement of children. It was distinctly unpleasant and disconcerting now. Jim was lost. He turned around desperately, confusing himself still more.

'Fucked if I know where we are,' he muttered.

'Keep cool,' Emma remarked.

Jim laughed, a note of hysteria in his voice. 'Cool? People have died of hypothermia and been far less cool.'

'Remember those clouds this morning?' Emma asked, apparently inconsequentially. Caught on the wrong footing, Jim nodded bemusedly.

'Well, they were snowclouds.'

'So?' Jim demanded nervously.

'They were the only clouds in the sky. Don't you see? They were due north . . . ish.'

Suddenly Jim did see. He interrupted, finishing off her train of thought: 'So that means that the wind could easily be in the north, and it's coming from . . .' he licked his finger and held it up in the air. After a moment he gesticulated over his right shoulder. ' . . . Over there. So that way,' he waved his hand in front and to the left, 'should be roughly south. Brilliant.' He took hold of Emma and gave her a huge kiss.

'So where now?' Emma asked at last. Jim frowned.

'It's too far to Inverie. Let's try to get back to Camusrory.'

'Where?'

'Camusrory, the bothy.'

'Fair enough.'

They ran again with new resolve and energy, side by side, across the moors. After about half an hour they both began to hear the beautiful, welcoming sound of waves washing on to a beach. It was the first sound they had heard in hours, barring any noise they had made themselves.

And even this noise seemed to be eternally saying 'Hush', and then drawing in its breath through pursed lips, then 'Hush' again. The ground began to flatten out and they found themselves on a peninsula, about the size of a small cricket pitch. A drystone dyke loomed up in front, low and ragged. They climbed over the tumbledown heap of stones and saw a ruined cottage in front. It was like seeing the gates of paradise after a millennia in purgatory.

'Thank Christ,' Jim said gladly. This place he recognized, although he had only ever seen it from the loch, somewhere on the far side. It was the northern point of the mouth they had come through that afternoon. They had run in a long arc, ending up only four or so miles from Camusrory, but goodness knows how many by the route they had blindly chosen.

They stumbled to the house and climbed through the holes that had once been windows. It was the last, darkest, coldest hour before dawn. They huddled together under the window. Snow was fluttering into the room above their heads and gathering in small drifts on the far side, by what had been an inside door.

'What now?' Emma asked through chattering teeth. Jim shook his head and moved one shoulder in an excuse for a shrug. The wind whistled and sighed among the threadbare pile of rocks that constituted the derelict bothy. The cold began to pass from being an intense, agonizing chill, which seemed to penetrate every bone to the marrow, every muscle, with shards of ice, to an almost sweet numbness. Clinging to each other like children, the two began to submerge into a comforting haze of sleep. Emma sank faster, for although she was strong she was not as physically and mentally tough as Jim. He fought the urge to sleep even as Emma embraced and welcomed it. She felt that she was walking towards a huge bonfire. She stumbled forward, stretching out her hands to allow the wonderful, revivifying heat into every pore in her body. Slowly, hesitantly she crept towards the crackling, roaring bonfire. It seemed to be so safe and beautiful . . . heavenly, even. 'If this were heaven,' a voice in her mind said, 'I'd be willing to stay here for an eternity and more.' But even as most of her mind bathed in the sweet warmth and pleaded for more, a nagging voice still fought on, saying: 'Resist, resist.' But she moved ever closer. A feeling of immense happiness flooded into her fuddled brain. She stretched, throwing back her head and smiling ecstatically. The nagging had receded to a distant whisper, and still she ignored it. She arched, spreadeagled, naked, inches from the fire in an ecstasy of abandon at this, her last and greatest orgasm of pleasure.

Then the fire began to recede. The tiny whimper, up until this moment cowed and defeated, gathered strength again, rallying and forcing back the fire. She cried out, an empty, infinitely desperate, plaintive cry as the fire died out and the cold began to gnaw again.

Jim had almost succumbed to sleep when the watery, grey light of dawn crawled over the mountains to the east like a wounded animal. It trickled into the small room, falling softly on the heap of snow which now covered the floor and illuminating the browned, quivering nettles which sprouted from between the rotting planks. Jim awoke and turned to Emma, seeing a smile on her face. Her hair was whitened with snow, frozen and brittle. Her face was like ivory, with vague hints of blue under her eyes and along the line of her cheekbones. She was barely breathing. Jim shook her with the violence of sudden fear, and a small, forlorn groan broke from her lips. Her head lolled back and her eyes remained closed; a single tear glistened as it trickled down her cheek, leaving a trail like the path of a snail across her face. He shook her even more viciously and she cried out, her eyes flickering open.

'Why?' she asked, her voice cracking with sorrow. Jim dragged her to her feet and she tottered unsteadily, swaying on legs that buckled with weakness.

'This'll be the death of you,' Jim muttered. He flexed his right hand and, turning her around roughly, he slapped her hard on the bottom. The method may have been crude but it worked. The force of the blow made his hand sting. Emma yelped like a whipped dog and leapt away from him, staring around wildly. She saw Jim, and the same innocent, defenceless look came into her eyes for the second time that night.

'I was having such a lovely dream. Why did you hit me?' The disjointed sentences and the tone were like those of a ten-year-old.

'You were dying of cold. That's how you die of hypothermia: sleep, sweet dreams and away you go.'

Emma shivered violently, her whole body joining in. The spasm passed and she yawned. 'If that's death, I think I prefer it.'

Jim smiled and hugged her. 'You may prefer it, but I don't,' he said into her ear.

'Well, I s'pose some day I'll thank God that you're selfish and possessive. But I'm not up to it at the moment . . . and besides, God's been on the blink lately.'

The snow was lying three inches deep outside the house. They walked out, back on to the hill, following the shoreline eastwards to Camusrory. As they trudged heavily along the tree-lined heights above the loch they supported each other. Jim hung the rifle upside-down beneath his left arm and held Emma around the waist with his right. Emma, in turn, had her right arm around Jim's shoulders, and was carrying the cocaine with the other, shifting it frequently when her arm or shoulder began to ache. Jim kept up a slow but regular pace, and they talked incessantly in a disjointed way. Occasionally Jim would point out a

47

mountain or a landmark as it drew level, as much to cheer himself as Emma.

'That's Seal Island down there,' he said at one point, nodding down to a small promontory dotted, it seemed, with large, smooth, rounded boulders. 'Can you see the seals?' he asked, in much the same way that a teacher would say to his pupils on a visit to the zoo: 'That's the elephant house. D'you see the big elephant?' . . . They were words, not instructive nor even particularly interesting, but useful in themselves just for being words.

After four hours of this they were on the top of a hill which overlooked the bothy. A fire sent a thin column of smoke spiralling into the low clouds. The lights were on. The bothy looked wonderfully inviting. A large trawler, bigger than *Rob Roy* and expensively equipped, lay at anchor off the jetty. It was the sort of intermediate trawler, bigger than the prawn boats but smaller than the ones which went in fleets far out into the Atlantic, designed for fishing deep waters for herring and mackerel.

Quietly Jim thanked God that they had returned before Ian. The thought of Ian running blindly into this nest of hornets had been worrying him ever since he woke up. The two people lay down in a peat hag, out of the icy wind, and watched the proceedings.

It was now obvious that whoever had tried to come on them by surprise had somehow known where to come and had fully expected to ambush whoever was there. After a few minutes of studying them through the telescopic sights of the rifle, his finger itching on the trigger when the bead passed over a defenceless, unsuspecting person, Jim realized with a certain amount of pleasure that the people below were confused and angry. At a guess there were not more than six of them inside the bungalow. One by one, and occasionally in pairs, they would wander outside with walkie-talkies, turning in various directions. Jim puzzled

48

himself by trying to work out what they were doing, his mind cold and not as clear as it usually was. It was Emma who, breaking their long silence, explained their actions.

'There're still some of them out on the hill.'

Jim nodded sagely, for a second pretending that, of course, he had known this all along. Then he thought better of his immediate reaction and murmured, 'You're right. Makes sense.'

It seemed, as the minutes struggled by, that a certain degree of strained impatience was creeping into the waiting people. They took to yelling out a string of names: 'Alan, Bill, Jock, Mac,' again and again. At first the two watchers were too far away to make out what was being shouted. But the degree of repetition was enough in itself, after a while to explain: there were four people missing, confirming Jim's initial guess that there were ten of them to start with. The impatience gradually turned to anger. People came and went from the bothy at shorter intervals and one man made an attempt to climb the hill on which the chase had begun. The depth of the heather and snow defeated him before he had gone thirty yards from the garden, and he turned back.

It was exactly forty-five minutes since Jim and Emma had started their vigil when one ragged figure stumbled up towards the house from the east, roughly from the northern spur of the mountain called Sgurr na Ciche. The two watchers on the hill saw him long before his friends did. He would stumble a few yards, then stop; then another few yards and another halt. As he came closer, Jim looked at him through the telescopic sight of his rifle and saw with grim pleasure that he was limping. The fool appeared to have gone out on to the hill in wellingtons, the worst possible footwear for cold weather. To make his predicament worse, he seemed to have lost one. His limping came into perspective when Jim saw his muddy and snow-frozen

49

besocked foot. It made Jim and Emma feel better just watching him. When he had about a hundred and fifty yards to go, some watcher spotted him. There was a shout and all six men ran out to help. As they reached him he collapsed, exhausted.

Seizing their chance the couple put into practice a half-formulated plan that they had agreed on. In a moment both were on their feet and bounding, at the crouch, down the hill. They vaulted the dyke and sprinted across the garden, keeping the bothy between them and their foes, and ending up breathless by the west wall of the bungalow. They sidled to the corner and peeped around it. The six men were still bending over their friend. Jim grabbed Emma's soaking sweater and almost dragged her the last thirty yards to the jetty. There was a small rubber dinghy, obviously the one that the men had used to land, and a bigger boat, wooden and equipped with wide-bladed oars. Quick as a flash Jim whipped out his knife and slashed at the dinghy. Then he jumped into the wooden boat, curled his fingers around the oar handles to get the feel of them, bent his back and expertly heaved the craft away from the shore, using a minimum of effort to cover the maximum distance, as any good oarsman can. When they were about a third of the way across, the men on the shore, a hundred yards away, at last spotted them. One shouldered his rifle and fired. For the distance between gun and moving target, it was a shot to be proud of. When they heard the report, Jim and Emma threw themselves into the bilge water, cold and stagnant in the bottom of the boat. As they moved, the bullet tore through the wood and whistled past within an inch of Emma's head. Luckily the trajectory was shallow from this distance: had the firer been a few yards higher up, the bullet would have hit Emma full in the body as she flung herself down. But it skimmed past her and punched through the far side of the boat, just below the waterline.

Water spurted in through the neat, round hole, soaking Emma's legs. They righted themselves and were clambering back on to the struts which passed for seats when a man came out on to the deck of the trawler.

In all the time that they had scanned the people below them they had not suspected that anyone was on the trawler: no light had been on, no person seen. When he appeared, Emma and Jim saw him simultaneously, although the latter was half-turned back towards the shore. With the coordination of instinctive reaction, Emma hauled on one oar and Jim dived for the rifle even as the man raised his own gun and fired. The bullet crashed into the wood where Jim had just been. But there was no time for a second attempt: already Jim had the rifle in one hand and, as the man fumbled with the bolt of his gun, Jim turned, firing from the hip. Despite the pitching of the boat and the lack of aiming, something found its mark. Four shots in rapid succession left Jim's gun. The attacker was hit by at least one. The force of the .303 bullet lifted him off his feet and hurled him across the deck. He fired off a wild shot as he fell, and that was the last thing he did. Emma stared agape at the crumpled body.

'Jim!' she screamed, aghast.

'Shut your fucking face!' he replied viciously. In a few oar strokes they were beside the trawler, and they clambered on board. Jim hauled in the anchor as the three fastest men reached the jetty and began to shoot. Bullets thumped into the trawler, splintering wood and exploding a pane of glass inwards. Emma ran towards cover, but as she reached the cabin one of the bullets found a mark. She was hit in the side with a shock which felt like she had been kicked by a horse. She was hurled across the planks, hitting her head hard as she fell. Jim leapt to her inert body, thinking for a split second of horror that she was dead. But she came

51

to, winded and gasping for breath, blood oozing from her side.

'I'm okay,' she wheezed, ' . . . only a scratch . . . Think it got the coke, though.' Her guess was right. Ironically her life had been saved by a sack of cocaine: it had taken the full force of the blast, like a protective sandbag. When Jim emptied the sack on to the deck three bags were damaged. The white substance poured from one into a small puddle, moistening to a glutinous, sticky heap.

Jim patted her and crawled back to the shore-facing side of the boat. The attackers had adopted tactical positions back on the shore: at least three were inside the house, one was behind the wooden struts which supported the jetty, and another was crawling towards a pile of logs, pushing his rifle in front of him. Jim reloaded his rifle and aimed. He was a good shot, capable of putting a neat hole through a stag's heart at a hundred yards, with open sights. Without any problem at all he could have killed two of his adversaries before they knew he was firing. But his intentions were more ambitious. He slipped off the safety catch and squeezed the trigger. In a dream he saw the man who had been crawling on the ground leap up, screaming and holding the shattered remains of one hand. It was a disgusting sight: the bullet had struck the middle of his right palm, blowing away his knuckles. Only his thumb remained intact; everything above that was a bloody mess, fingers hanging off like dead branches at impossible, crazy angles. Jim retched. He crawled back from the edge and spoke to Emma, who was wincing as she stuck a handkerchief into the hole in her side.

'Could you drive this thing?'

'Course.'

'Are you okay?'

'Sure.'

'Really?'

52

'Really.' She stood up, the blood running down her side, and lurched into the cabin. A moment later the boat spluttered into life. The gunfire from the shore redoubled, now concentrated on the cabin. Glass shattered, the wooden walls were riddled, but Emma continued to turn the boat out into the loch. Jim reloaded his rifle, cramming ten bullets into the magazine and one into the breech. He took a deep breath, steeled himself and knelt up, firing as he rose. His bullets sprayed into the bothy, keeping their heads down and drawing the fire of the other two people. When he had emptied the magazine Jim ducked, frantically reloading. The distance from shore was increasing as Emma swerved the trawler away. But still bullets were striking the wood of the cabin above Jim's head with disturbing regularity. At last the magazine was full and Jim popped up again. It took a brief millisecond to get his bearings. The jetty was almost astern. Jim slewed around and emptied the entire magazine wildly at the man underneath the jetty, who was at least twenty yards nearer than his friends. He noticed with grim satisfaction that no more shots came from that direction. A moment later this was confirmed when a man staggered out into the open, blood gushing from a messy wound below his left shoulder.

'Mutton,' Jim muttered. Stags, he knew from years of experience, often move spasmodically when shot through the heart, then die. For a second it occurred to Jim that it was peculiar that men and animals react similarly when shot, then he pushed the thought from his mind. The man stumbled to the edge of the loch and collapsed, face down, half in the water.

Then the battle was over. It had taken no more than five minutes to change Jim's and Emma's lives, turning upside-down everything from which they derived stability. Two men lay dead, another was badly wounded, Emma had been hit – not badly, but not just grazed either. And, as Jim wandered back to the cabin, he noticed something on his shoulder. Absentmindedly he brushed at it and searing pain ran down his arm. A shard of wood, tapering and long, had embedded itself like a dagger in his right shoulder. He took it in his left hand, gritted his teeth and twisted it out. Warm blood flowed out, sticky and steaming, and ran down his chest. As he walked into the cabin Emma looked up, her face contorted in her attempt to hold down her emotions.

'Should I congratulate you or disown you?' she asked with a humourless smile.

Jim sat down heavily and let his rifle clatter to the floor. He looked around dispassionately. The place was pockmarked with bullet holes. The table that Emma had turned over to hide behind during the gunfight had three round holes in it. By some fluke Emma had escaped without further wounds. She had removed her sweater and was wearing only a white tee-shirt which was torn on the right side and drenched with blood. The bullet had punched through the sack of cocaine, entering her midriff with its velocity all but spent. Even so its remaining force had carried it into her back just below the ribcage, tearing through flesh and muscle before it got there. On inspection Jim saw that already a huge, purple-black bruise was spreading under her skin around the slight bump which was the snub nose of the bullet. Luckily it had not been a hollow shell, or a lead one, which would have expanded and splintered on impact. But then if it had been, Jim found himself speculating with surprising dispassion, it would probably have done much more damage to the sack of cocaine without ever going near her body . . . And as it was the coke which had got them in this position in the first place, it would have been a bit of a shame if . . .

Jim shook his head sharply, cutting off the unwanted thought in mid-flow.

'Both,' he finally answered her question.

'Doesn't leave much room for sitting down and talking this out like civilized humans, does it?' she remarked. 'Three still missing, likely dead, on the moor; one more, I'd say, with severe frostbite. One man dead with bullets from your rifle, and one more wounded. To make matters worse the dead one's on the boat we've just stolen.'

'One more dead,' Jim added.

Emma laughed wildly. 'Oh really?' she all but shrieked. 'Fab. Fucking wonderful. What's one man in a war . . . ?' She looked at him with mock seriousness. 'What's it like to be a multiple murderer?'

'D'you think I enjoyed it?' Jim retorted.

'*I don't fucking know*!' The emotion began to pour out. Tears streamed down her face.

'I didn't. Don't you think it's enough of a burden to carry without you freaking out too?'

'I'm not freaking out. I'm just shocked at the apparent simplicity and ease with which you killed someone.'

'Oh, for Christ's sake!' Now Jim was losing his temper. 'Cool down, will you . . . !' He could not bear having this fight. He already felt emotionally as well as physically shattered. His state of mind transcended disgust and horror at what he had just seen and done. He felt as if someone had taken the plug out of sanity and everything was suddenly turning into a terrible, lunatic nightmare with him as the main protagonist.

'Cool?' Emma remarked, dangerously calm. 'Cool . . . Ah yes, the elixir for all evils. Keep cool and everything's hunky-bloody-dory.' She stopped, suddenly sobered from her momentary madness. Pain throbbed in her side, her head ached, and when she glanced at the floor she saw that the planks were glistening and slippery with their mingled blood. It had always interested her how it felt to be shot in cold blood, like in the movies. She knew now

55

that when it hits you it is like being struck by a piledriver. Then surprise and shock briefly flash through your mind before the pain obliterates all other thoughts. Humans invariably believe that their supreme status on earth renders them invulnerable. In so-called civilized people the knowledge of death has very nearly disappeared: it takes a close-hand experience of the bestial side of human nature to realize that we are, in fact, very vulnerable indeed. Even then the shock of realization is immense. Emma was as amazed and scared as she was in pain. She shook her head and groaned.

'Shit, what a mess.' There was deliberate ambiguity in this statement: their safe, happy lives were like the cabin in which they sat . . . shot to ribbons. How they would get out of this hardly bore contemplation.

She steered the boat on in silence, slowly up the loch. Jim was also very quiet. He was studying the wound on his shoulder with distaste.

'Here comes Ian. Punctual as ever,' Emma said, breaking the silence for the first time in some minutes. Jim stood up and saw *Rob Roy* coming around the head of the loch, hugging the shore. He went out on deck and waved with his good arm. *Rob Roy* turned and cut across the loch. It came up beside and both boats stopped, their anchors clattering in unison as they sank to the shallow floor of the loch. Moments later Ian appeared and walked over to where Jim was already waiting for him. He studied Jim, frowning.

'You look terrible,' he remarked helpfully.

'I don't feel all that rosy.'

Ian climbed on to the bigger boat and sat down on the side while Jim told him what had happened. He recounted the events in succinct, curt sentences, too tired to elaborate any more than was necessary. Ian listened in silence until he had finished. Then he bit his lip and looked around.

56

'Well,' he said with a small smile, 'at least yer alive.'

Jim snorted. 'Just.'

'Aye well, but it could be worse though . . . Onywise, I cannae say I've had as much fun as you two, but my news is that the polis are aifter us. God knows how they ken . . . but they're saying in Mallaig that the Big Boy's been in cahoots wi' them fer months.'

'Which Big Boy?' Jim asked.

Ian slapped his leg. 'Och . . . sorry, I forgot tae tell you. Thon boat we saw the ither nicht belongs tae the guy whae bought Skelsay last summer. I cannae remember his name off hand, but . . .'

'Stevens. Sir Roy Stevens,' Jim cut in.

'Aye. Thon's the man.'

Jim frowned, wrinkling his nose in disbelief. 'Can't be,' he said under his breath.

'Mebbe it is, mebbe it's no. But thon's whit they're saying in Mallaig . . . and Oban, too. Fact everyone but us seems to have kent it since afore Christmas.'

'But Stevens is a big shot. Industrialist or something. He's too straight to be dealing in coke.'

'More fool you fer believing it.'

'But that means he's behind the animals that just tried to kill us. We should go to the police.'

Ian laughed drily at this. 'The polis in Mallaig cannae tell their cocks frae their fingers, you should know that. And the yins doon in Oban and even in Glesgae, he's got in his jacket pocket.'

'What do we do, then?' This was not so much a question as a plea for help.

'Split up an' run fer it,' Ian replied.

He even had a plan, which he had worked out some-where between Mallaig and here. The presence of a second boat made matters considerably easier. Secretly, far below his uncompromising surface, Ian loved Jim and Emma as his children, as well as his protégés. He knew they would be safer on the sea than anywhere else. The only person he could think of who could better Jim in this part of the world was himself; so, as long as they stuck inside the archipelago, it would take a fleet to catch them.

His plan was simple. One boat should head north, the other south. Thereafter they would both be on their own. They would communicate through the local fishermen's radio station, Radio North-West, which was just a glorified CB terminal. That airwave would treat them as a priority and warn other fishermen where they were, when they were in danger, when they needed something, and so on. This was an enormously useful advantage to have. It was one of the perks of their notoriety that they could rely on such things.

For the most part Jim and then Emma approved of the plan. It was simple, uncomplicated and as safe as anywhere else was likely to be. They even had the benefit of being able to take the initiative and get a start. In fact their only disagreement was over how they should refer to their boats over the airwaves. Jim and Ian had agreed on a name for the stolen trawler, but Ian subbornly refused to call *Rob Roy* anything else than *Rob Roy*. Jim said that this was stupid and Ian replied that he had 'niver changed her name in forty years, and I'm no daeing it now.'

In the end Jim capitulated. He was too tired to argue.

Side by side the two boats crossed Loch Nevis and swung past the headlands and into the Sound of Sleat. What was inevitably snow up in the hills was falling on to the sea as a fine, cold drizzle. The sea was choppy but not uncomfortable. Waiting, a mile out into the sea, was a single police boat. The two trawlers headed straight for it, twenty yards apart, confusing it with two options rather than the single one it had expected. When they were almost on top of it Ian waved to Jim and both trawlers swerved away at a

58

steady forty-five degrees to each other. For almost a minute the police boat hovered as its captain went through the lengthy and arduous procedure of receiving new orders from Mallaig. Then it picked on the smaller of the two and gave chase. *Rob Roy* lurched into overdrive and headed away south towards Eigg. Jim turned his boat away in a leisurely fashion and set course for Loch Alsh.

'Will he get caught?' Emma asked. She was lying on the table which she had righted a few minutes before.

'Doubt it,' Jim answered from the controls. 'He's been playing cat and mouse with the fuzz since he was twenty. He's near on sixty now.'

Satisfied, Emma slid on to a stool. Any movement which tightened the skin down her right side brought a renewed bout of bleeding. She was in considerable pain – more pain, in fact, than she could ever remember feeling at one time. As they fled northwards her mood altered gradually from one of pained self-pity to contemplating the pile of cocaine which lay on the floor where it had been discarded in the heat of the battle. The more she stared at it, the more need stirred in her bones, where she had thought that there was no more need. Almost without realizing what her mind was doing she slipped into remembering the delicious, tingling, half-painful, half wonderfully sensual experience of cocaine in her nostrils and the feeling of light-hearted wellbeing as it flooded through her veins and into her mind.

With sudden amazement she realized how far this daydream had got out of hand. Her conscious rational half fought back, attempting to dam this unsavoury flood of remembrances with arguments of addiction and ill-gotten pleasures. But the more she stared the further away those arguments receded. It was with wonder that she heard her own voice speaking very clearly, somewhere inside her head.

59

'It's been in front of me for two days now. Temptation beyond endurance . . . Just a little bit can't do any harm.'

She reached out and picked up one of the small bags, knowing that one taste would be enough to destroy years of hard-won abstention, but it did not seem to matter. In a trance she poured some of the white substance from the split bag on to the table. She took the sheath knife from her belt and slowly stroked, caressed the dust into a level covering. This she cut into two halves and then proceeded to even one of these out into a neat line. She would cut it, stroke it into a line again, cut it again, stroke, cut, stroke, cut, stroke . . . until a perfect line stretched away in front of her. Then she moved on to the second half. It was a careful, laborious process, done with the loving precision of an artist. After about ten minutes the drug lay in two neat, white lines: straight, parallel, about two inches from each other. She put down the knife and, after rummaging in her pocket a bit, produced a crumpled Clydesdale Bank pound note. She smoothed it out, noticing the pictures on both sides and studying them with a look of vague puzzlement, her eyebrows drawn together. Then she rolled it into a tube and stuck one end up her left nostril. She twitched her nose and slowly lowered the other end to the nearest of the two lines. She took a deep breath, exhaled an even deeper one and, putting a finger to her other nostril to block it, inhaled, sucking the substance up her nose. She moved the tube up the line, meticulously hoovering up every last particle. Her head twitched to one side, a spasm of mixed pain and delight passing across her face. Then she snorted in air to clear the nostril and lay back, slowly letting her eyes droop shut.

After what seemed like a lifetime of ecstasy she awoke and stared at Jim's back, all stained on one side with his blood.

'Jim?' The word came out soft and indistinct.

'Jim?' louder this time.

'Mm?'

'How're you feeling?'

'Dead.'

'Does your arm hurt?'

'Yes.'

She stopped, carefully choosing the correct words. She wanted to tempt him, rather than frighten him away.

'I could make you feel better.'

Jim laughed drily. 'Mebbe . . .' he said, mimicking Ian, 'mebbe no . . . How much audience participation does it involve?'

'Only a little.'

Again he laughed, or at least allowed a short snort to leave his nose in an excuse for mirth. 'Then it's not what I thought it was.'

The subtle approach, evidently, was not working. Jim had a habit of running verbal circles around people at the best of times. This was not, by any stretch of the imagination, one of those. Emma opted for a more straightforward approach.

'Take some coke. It'll make you feel better.'

'Will it?' There was a hint of sarcasm behind this simple question.

'I swear it.'

After a brief pause he spoke again. 'Presumably you have and do?'

'Sorry?'

'You *have* taken some and do feel better!' he explained.

'Yes, on both counts.'

'Aye, aye.'

The silence that followed was very long. They were passing through Kyle Rhea, the strait between the Sound of Sleat and Loch Alsh.

'Drink and make merry . . .' Emma said at last.

61

' . . . for tomorrow you die,' Jim finished the sentence quickly. 'Don't stop for me.'

'So you won't have some?' Emma asked. He shook his head. Emma looked at his back for a moment and then she seemed to come to a decision. Picking up the pound note from where she had discarded it she snorted the second line.

For a while she talked, apparently unconcerned at the total lack of response from Jim. Her mind flickered through a series of thoughts which made very little sense and only appeared to be connected in the convoluted muddle of her fuddled brain.

Finally Jim tired of this incessant babble. 'Could you do me a favour?' he asked.

She stopped in mid-sentence. 'Sure. What?'

'Could you fix me something to eat?'

'Oh,' she said, as if slightly confused. 'I'm not really very hungry.'

Jim laughed quickly. 'I guessed that.'

Emma thought about this for a moment and then stood up, smiling to herself, and went down to the small kitchen. Jim heard sounds of clanking and banging below in the kitchen, with a few hearty curses thrown in. He smiled. The pain in his shoulder was still nagging him but he felt better. It was as if a door had instinctively closed in his mind, shutting off the unwanted horror he had felt back in Loch Nevis. All in all, he thought, things could have been worse . . . far worse. Against some odds he himself and Ian and – almost more important than both put together – Emma, were all alive. That was enough.

Emma reappeared carrying a tray. On it was a bowl of steaming soup, a plate of baked beans on toast and a mug of black coffee. Her meal consisted of a can of lager and a cigarette.

Jim kissed her and, putting the boat into its lowest gear

and setting the wheel straight, attacked his first meal in almost two days. When he had finished he stood up stiffly and carried his coffee to the controls, balancing it on one upraised knee and lighting a cigarette.

'I think I can face the world now,' he said over his shoulder, grinning.

'Same here,' she replied. 'Wish I'd stop bleeding, though.'

'Wonder how Ian fared?' Jim asked, posing the question to himself as much as to Emma.

She shrugged and stood up unsteadily, turned on the wireless set and put one earphone to her ear. After some delicate twiddling she found the correct channel and unplugged the headset, flooding the room with a pop song, heavy and tuneless. She picked up the receiver and covered the mouthpiece. 'What's our codename?' she whispered.

'*Blue Dog*.' They both smiled. It was the name of a pub in London notorious as a watering hole for society junkies.

Emma took her hand from the mouthpiece and spoke quietly into it.

'*Blue Dog* to pirate, *Blue Dog* to pirate, do you read me? Come in pirate, over.'

'Hearing you loud as a bell, *Blue Dog*.' A woman's voice came back, with the soft lilting highland accent.

'We're about two miles short of the Kyle of Loch Alsh, heading for . . .' She looked back at Jim enquiringly.

'Tarbert . . . Harris,' he said, adding the name of the island when she did not seem to register the first name.

'Sorry, Pirate. We're headed for Tarbert. Any news of *Rob Roy*? Over.'

'Wait and see, over.'

Emma hung up the mouthpiece and sat down. The song came to a bashing, jangling climax and began to fade out. What sounded like a massed pipe band was faded in over the top. The tune was 'Over the Sea to Skye'. The same soft, lilting voice that Emma had just heard spoke silkily over the tune.

'We've just had a *Blue Dog* on the line. Keep your eyes out if you're in the Little Minch or Tarbert.' She continued, listing a series of codenames and their whereabouts, and warning of evil currents off Uist. Also, she said, five sea-pigs, or police launches, had just left Oban. At the very end of the interlude, as the pipe band was beginning to fade, she gave the news that not only *Blue Dog* but also half of the fishermen in the Western Isles were waiting to hear.

'Oh yes. There was a right old cat and mouse around Skye today. As they say, the older the better. And to prove it old *Rob Roy* gave them the slip off Soay this afternoon.' She switched on and off one of those studio gimmick-noises that disc jockeys always use, a huge cheer in this case. Then the next song began.

'Good,' Jim remarked, standing up. He leant close to the bridge screen to see his way through the narrows off Kyle of Lochalsh in the gathering dusk. There were lights kept to the right of this, hugging the mainland point called the Plock of Kyle a name which had always for some unknown reason, amused him. Then he set course for the gap in between Cravlon Island and Longay, remembering with sudden apprehension that Skelsay was now very close by. The thought of passing so close to the hornet's nest, if Ian was to be believed, did not amuse him one jot. In her chair Emma slowly sank down, sagging, until her head gently met with the table. She slept.

The weather, out of the sheltered sound behind Skye, rapidly became rough. Although the wind was not particularly strong the drizzle lost no time in turning into a proper west-coast downpour. By the time they had passed Raasay, dim and low against the black, brooding Cuillins of southern Skye, the droplets of rain were ricocheting off the deck and bridge screen like small tennis balls.

Jim was unperturbed. He held his course along the coast, passing the mountains of Wester Ross and the sea lochs of Torridon and Gairloch before cutting east, around the headland of Rubha Reidh. By then he was almost asleep. He had caught himself as he dropped three times in the previous hour and was not willing to risk being in that condition when he attempted the dangerous island-dotted, evil-currented Bay of Annat and Loch Broom. He walked across to Emma and shook her.

She was wide awake in a moment.

'Yes?'

'Could you steer?'

'Sure . . . where are we?' She looked at her watch and then glanced out of the window, frowning. There was still land to the right, which meant that they were not where they should have been by that time.

'Just beyond Rubha Reidh.'

Emma yawned, still not fully awake.

'Where's that? This isn't the Minch.'

'It is, just not the part we were going to be on.'

'Oh? So where are we going?'

'Ullapool.'

Emma smiled, at last understanding what Jim was saying.

'Not so stupid.' She walked to the controls and sat down, rubbing her eyes with her knuckles. A moment later she turned to ask Jim whether to hug the mainland or steer out into the bay. But he was already asleep. She sighed and chose the second, safer course. The radio whispered behind her, keeping her awake but not breaking her concentration. She steered out, wide around Greenstone Point and towards Priest Island, in the centre of the bay.

65

Two trawlers went by, heading out into the open sea. Emma radioed them.

'*Blue Dog* to whoever, d'you read?' she said quietly, dropping her voice half an octave.

'We read you, *Blue Dog* . . . You'll be taking the long road tae Harris, or you'll be lost.' A typically polite western way of saying, 'What the hell are *you* doing here?'

Emma snorted. 'No, we're not lost, we're headed for Ullapool.'

'No! Chust a pretty face, young Robert MacGregor?'

Emma muttered, 'If only you knew, babe,' as she hung up the mouthpiece. With that they parted, two cutting away to the north-west, the other holding a steady northeast.

It was pitch dark when the small islands which guarded and confused the mouth of Loch Broom began to loom up ahead. Jim had been asleep for under an hour, but Emma knew that she could not navigate the islands. She let the boat slow almost to a halt, rocking on the surge. Then she stood up and walked over to Jim. His head lay, cheek down, on the table. One arm was thrust out, lying limp behind his head, the other swung idly beside his chair. His face was peaceful and calm, his mouth slightly open and his breathing deep and regular. For a moment Emma hesitated, unwilling to disturb his hard-earned rest. Then she spoke quietly.

'Jim?'

His eyes flickered open. 'Mmm?'

'You'll have to steer, my love.'

He yawned cavernously, screwing up his eyes and letting the breath out for a remarkably long time, in a sort of half-sigh.

'Sure.' He slowly gathered himself, climbed off the chair and stood for a moment, waving like a reed in the breeze. He clenched his eyes shut and shook his head violently.

The giddiness quickly passed, leaving him with a faint nausea. Swearing under his breath he headed back to the controls and slid into the seat.

'Could do with a cup of coffee.'

'Your wish is my command,' Emma answered with a smile.

As he navigated the bay, letting experience and long knowledge do the majority of the work, he remembered with disgust the gun battle. The blood of a man he had never talked to, let alone known his name, stained the deck. That man would never be buried, his family would never know what had happened to him and would invent some noble story of dying at sea. It was perhaps a small mercy that they did not know that he had been a thug who had come out of a gun battle as the loser and had been dumped unceremoniously into Loch Nevis, with a spare anchor tied to his leg.

Emma brought up two cups of coffee and placed one in front of Jim. She retreated, tousling his salt-stiff hair absentmindedly as he moved back. The surge of thoughts retreated into the darker corners of Jim's subconscious as he carefully steered around a submerged reef which surrounded a tiny island. The reef constituted the sole reason why Bottle Island was worthy of naming. It took half an hour to negotiate the islands, then they were into the mouth of Loch Broom. The moon momentarily appeared from behind the scudding clouds. It was a night off full, bright and clear, its craters showing like pockmarks in a round cheese with one corner cut off. Away to the left, on Coigach, Ben More glowered darkly out to sea.

Jim swung *Blue Dog* down the middle of the loch and soon the lights of Ullapool appeared in front – row upon row of friendly, homely lights. A minute later the beacon at the mouth of the harbour appeared, an inviting, beckoning green spot in the inky darkness.

They edged into the harbour and steered across to a jetty with a spare berth between two larger trawlers, where *Blue Dog* could hide. They tied up the boat and were inspecting one of the many bullet holes when a voice spoke from above.

'You must be the *Blue Dog*.' They looked up but the speaker was obscured in darkness behind a torch he was pointing at them. He had a strong Glaswegian accent. Jim and Emma looked up warily.

'What if we are?' said Emma, with a hint of threat in her voice which belied her sudden fear.

'If you are . . .' the speaker answered, turning the torch slowly towards himself, ' . . . if you are then Ullapool's with you.'

To their relief the man was wearing wellingtons and an oilskin overcoat which hung down to his thighs.

'I'm the local hero round here,' he said, identifying himself as the publican, 'and there's a free drink for you at the Fishermen's Return.'

Emma looked at Jim and he smiled back, shrugging his shoulders.

'Why not?' he asked. Emma's smile broadened. She walked slowly up the stone staircase to the jetty, leaning heavily against the wall with an outstretched hand. Jim followed.

Ten minutes later they were sitting beside the coal fire of a warm, comfortable pub. Triple whiskies sat on the table in front of them. A small group of gnarled old men, their faces puckered and bronzed by the elements, sat at the bar watching the couple out of the corners of their eyes. The publican came across to them with a newspaper and sat down. Emma slowly reached out, hesitated for a moment over her glass and then opted for the newspaper, which the man had pointedly dropped on to the table. It was *The Western Gazette*, showing on the front a hazy picture

68

of *Rob Roy* in Oban harbour. The main article was dramatically entitled Death on the High Seas. It was, despite its name, a humdrum, ill-informed and badly written article, based on guesswork and a fair amount of invention. Emma read it to herself, smiling faintly at certain passages and then read it aloud to Jim.

It was a short piece which, in fact, only succeeded in informing the readers that two boats were being looked for in connection with a large haul of drugs and a double murder. The fierce gun battle by the bothy of Camusrory was referred to with awe as a 'western-style shoot-out'. But, judging by the facts that the police had actually allowed to be put into print, the shoot-out might as well have been an unfortunate accident.

Other than that Ian was both named and described, Jim was accurately described and Emma was guessed at. Her disguise had proved useful. When she had finished reading Emma put down the newspaper and took a large swig from her glass.

'They're going to be muddled about you,' Jim remarked quietly. Emma threw back a wolfish grin in answer. After a brief silence the publican plucked up his courage and cleared his throat.

'Is . . . is it true?' he asked, nodding towards the paper. Jim and Emma, lost in their private thoughts, did not appear to hear the question. Then Jim looked up.

'What? . . . Oh that . . . some of it.'

'The bit about the shoot-out?'

'Not entirely,' Jim replied evasively.

'Did you kill one of them, though?'

'They started it,' Emma put in, with a wry smile. There was another brief silence. The people at the bar were desperately trying to pretend that they were not listening. They were speaking in short, disjointed sentences and leaning back on their stools, attempting to pick up every

69

word of the *sotto voce* conversation on the other side of the room.

'Yes,' Jim answered at last, deciding that the time for pretence was over. It had not lasted long, but that was to be expected. A bunch of liars to the man, the west-coasters knew the truth when they saw it and respected it in circumstances such as this, or at least this is what Jim had hoped. Besides, there are other ways of killing a cat than clubbing it to death.

'I killed two of them.' There were a few mutters and the gruff hissing of whispers from the bar. ' . . . It was them or us . . .' He stopped and put his head in his hands. Although it was a subject that little amused Emma she had to take a sip of whisky to conceal an involuntary smile. If anyone knew a clever, subtle method for killing cats, Jim did.

'Dinnae fret yersel, man. We're on your side.'

They stayed in Ullapool for two nights and a full day. When they awoke in the two beds the landlord had found for them it was after midday; they had slept for fourteen hours. They ate a hearty breakfast of eggs, fried bread, bacon, sausages, black pudding and porage, whilst trying to hide the blood they had both shed on the linen sheets from the woman who brought their trays.

The publican appeared at two in the afternoon with a tall, middle-aged man who was evidently the doctor. He was thin, bordering on gaunt, with a long face, an aquiline nose and half-moon spectacles which sat halfway down the curved bridge of his nose. He had a look of being vaguely hassled, but not unduly so.

First he ordered Emma to strip to the waist. Emma stalled him until the landlord became restless and left the room. Then Jim tiptoed to the door and locked it as Emma peeled off her sweater and tee-shirt, revealing unquestionably that she was not the man people thought she was. The doctor, to his eternal credit, appeared to be imperturbable.

He did not bat an eyelid. His eyebrows rose fractionally, then he went to work without further ado. He prodded, squeezed and poked her. Sometimes she sat still, often however she winced and once she gasped, biting her lip against the pain.

'That hurt?' the doctor asked.

'Like hell.'

'Does it hurt to breathe?'

'A bit.'

'And to cough?'

'A bit more.'

After some more prodding around he moved away, rubbing his eyes below the lenses of his glasses. When he turned back they were watering, giving the peculiar effect of both magnifying and distorting his pupils.

'You've been lucky, my girl.' He frowned. Then one corner of his mouth curled up, ' . . . Or should I say, my boy . . . Anyway, you've been damned lucky. I'm not saying that there's no danger of haemorrhaging in there. Quite a lot of blood has accumulated under the skin already. And you've lost quite a bit of blood, though the bullet missed anything important. It could've fairly ripped out your lung, it could've torn out half of your guts, or smashed up your ribs, but it didn't. I'm buggered if I know what to do about that wound, though.'

'Couldn't you just hoik the bullet out and stitch her up?' Jim offered.

'I could,' the doctor replied uncertainly. 'But I'm loathe to do anything so drastic this soon. It'd be a wee bit like selling your car 'cos it's run out o' petrol.'

'What d'you mean?' Jim asked.

'Well . . . Thing is, there's one or two other things I

71

could do which'd be a damned sight better for it. But I'm afraid it'd take time.'

'And meanwhile I'll just go on bleeding to death over here while you two discuss me as if I was next Sunday's roast,' Emma remarked from her prostrate position on the bed. 'For Christ's sake just do whatever you have to do, but do it now.'

The doctor thought for a moment and frowned again. Finally he shrugged and sighed. 'Well,' he said unsurely, 'I s'pose it'd not be breaking my Hippocratic oath to take that bullet out and sew up the holes, and it'd certainly be quickest that way, but I'd rather . . .'

'Just do it,' Emma ordered through clenched teeth.

'But it's not the . . .'

'*Do it.*' she snapped. 'We're wanted on charges of multiple murder, drug smuggling and burglary already. By tomorrow morning they'll have thrown in rape, child-molesting, kidnapping and high treason, so get on with it.'

The doctor shrugged and rummaged around in his black bag, muttering to himself.

'What're you waiting for?' Emma asked as she could not see what was going on.

'I'm looking for something to anaesthetize you with!'

'Just get on with it, will you.'

He shrugged again. Then he took the lid off a brown bottle and tipped it on to a large ball of cotton wool, staining the latter yellow. He put down the bottle and walked to Emma's side, gave her an injection and then doused the wound with the cotton wool.

'Brace yourself,' he said, rubbing his hands.

He picked up a long scalpel which glinted as it caught the light, tested it by running it very gently over the back of his hand then, apparently satisfied, leant down close over Emma's back and lowered the blade to her skin.

'This might hurt a wee bit,' he said, and gently parted

the flesh which covered the bullet with the tip of the razor-sharp blade. The muscles on her back went taut, tight as ropes. The doctor straightened slowly, watching the newly freed reservoir of blood flow over her white skin, around her side and on to the linen, where it formed in a small crimson puddle.

'Aaaah . . .' he said under his breath. 'And there's the wee beastie.'

He rummaged in his black bag, produced a large pair of tweezers and leant over the wound again.

'You brave?' he inquired.

'Lioness,' came the muffled reply

'Good,' he said, 'then be brave now.'

He squinted down at the wound, an incision about an inch long.

'Okay,' he muttered. The tips of his tweezers entered Emma's flesh and slowly, carefully worked their way into a position from which they could gain a firm grip on the bullet. After what seemed like an age to Emma this was done and the doctor was ready to pull it out.

'One . . . two . . . three . . . and . . .' He twisted out the tweezers and Emma's back arched, instinctively compensating for the pain of the bullet tearing through her tender flesh. She bit the pillow but a muffled shriek escaped. The blood flowed out freely and the doctor doused it with the ball of cotton wool. Again she yelled out in agony.

'What the fuck're you doing?'

'Just cleaning up.'

'Well it sodding hurts.'

'Some might say it serves you right for getting yourself into this fix in the first place.'

'They'd be killjoys.' Jim laughed. Emma started to laugh too but the pain it brought on made it more trouble than the joke was worth.

The doctor stitched up her wound and bandaged her tightly. He stepped back, admiring his handiwork.

'I s'pose I couldn't prevail on you to lie up for a week or so?' he asked hopefully.

The answer Emma gave him was unexpectedly unsure. 'Is it bad, my wound?'

'No, not bad. But you've taken hurt all the same, and lost some blood, too. Those stitches are strong but they're not miraculous; neither are you, come to that. You'll be weak, getting weaker the longer you keep moving around. Also the stitches'll break or dissolve after a while, then you'll be back to square one. I'm not saying that your condition'll ever get dangerous, just that you'll be far more weak and prone to colds, flu, exhaustion than you'd normally be.'

'I can't stay,' Emma said, still not sounding positive.

'Stay if you want, I can do this alone, they'll follow me.' There was no anger of frustration in Jim's offer. It was entirely generous – Emma knew immediately that he would sorely miss her, but he was also willing to do anything that would be for her own good. Ironically it was this generosity that decided her against lying up in Ullapool; attractive though the offer was she could not leave Jim alone; he needed her and, more importantly, no wound could decrease her need for him. They were like two halves of the same whole.

'I'll go with Jim,' she said quietly, looking over towards her lover. She saw a faint flicker of joy pass through his eyes.

'Aye well. Nobody can say I didn't try,' the doctor muttered.

He moved to Jim. After a moment of probing he laughed. 'Feel like going back to Loch Nevis?' he asked.

'No, why?'

'Cos there's a wee bit of shoulder bone there somewhere

74

with your name on it.' He allowed himself a grin. 'Just a wee chip, though. Nothing much I can do but clean up the wound a bit.'

Jim laughed and looked at his shoulder. 'Just a wee chip . . . story of my life.'

The doctor turned to Emma who was now lying on her good side, watching the proceedings. 'I feed the lines, everyone else gets the laughs.'

Emma smiled reassuringly. 'There, there,' she said soothingly.

The doctor opened his mouth in a broad, kind, wry smile. Then he turned back and went to work on Jim's shoulder.

It was almost four hours since he had come in when the doctor finished his task. He washed his hands in the small, dirty basin and walked to his bag. He produced two bottles of pills and a brown, unlabelled bottle.

'These are painkillers,' he said, raising one of the pill bottles and then placing it on the table. 'And these are vitamins, sort of healthy pep pills . . .' He showed the second pill bottle and then put it beside the first. ' . . . And this' – he smiled slightly – 'is a small concoction of my own making. Be careful with it and only use it in extremities.'

'What's in it?' Jim asked.

'Mainly morphine . . . Doesn't go well with cocaine.'

This amazed Emma and Jim. Their faces must have betrayed their surprise because the doctor laughed.

'I may be an old yokel-doctor, but I'm not a complete fool. And if I've learnt one thing from living forty years amongst these uncouth West Highlanders, it's that temptation nearly always prevails in the end . . . I don't like the idea of you two taking that stuff because I think you're worth a bit more, but if it makes you keep going, which it surely will – for a while – then at least it has some point.'

Silence fell as the doctor packed his stuff and closed his case.

At last Jim spoke, his voice strained with emotion. 'Thank you, doctor. You've done us both a great favour and I won't forget it . . . Thank you.'

The doctor snorted and looked out of the window. It was dark outside and the harbour was busy with jostling, shouting fishermen. 'I've done no more than anyone else in the Western Isles would have done. Give it a week and people'll be clamouring to help you . . . Which makes them and me almost as big fools as you two.'

He added the twist to dilute his first sentence. It was a well-judged, astute remark that was to be proved true as Jim and Emma continued their run.

The doctor walked to the door, turned the handle and spoke over his shoulder. 'It'll be opening time downstairs . . . not that it ever isn't. Who's for a drink?'

'Me,' they answered together, like children being asked which one would like to go to the cinema.

Both men helped Emma down the stairs and into a comfortable armchair in a dark corner of the bar. The publican pulled up a table and chairs and took their orders while Jim and the doctor sat down. They had a drink and talked quietly. Then they had another drink, continuing their quiet conversation. Then they had yet another drink, raising their voices over the gathering hubbub in the bar. They remained anonymous, drinking away the pain with neat whisky while they conversed knowledgeably about politics, the weather, religion, the weather and the medical profession . . . and, of course, the weather.

All in all it was a fairly typical, long, amusing Western Isles conversation. Time passed surprisingly quickly. Suddenly it was ten o'clock and some of the earlier starters were beginning to trickle out on to the streets, supporting each other and laughing uproariously. There they gathered in an elegant, well-ordered row at the edge of the harbour and pissed into the water, talking animatedly about the weather and other amusing topics as they stood. In fact some of the funniest jokes heard all night, it seemed, were told as the men rid themselves of seven pints with whisky chasers.

At half-past ten two policemen walked into the bar. The sudden hush and the quickly exchanged glances told as clearly as any words that these were not friends.

The doctor leant over as the noise returned and whispered conspiratorially. 'Foreigners.' This meant that they were not from Ullapool.

As the policemen relished the discomfort and animosity they aroused even before they reached the bar, it was remarkable how a new, larger, noisier group built up round the table where the three were drinking, a barricade of bodies. Emma and Jim had naively thought that they were just more strangers, but it suddenly dawned on them that everyone had known who they were all along, and had left them alone until it was absolutely necessary to guard them. The Scots may have a reputation for being reticent and dour, but they know how to keep a secret.

' . . . Aye, they were caught in Tarbert, seemingly,' one of the boys in blue remarked, deliberately raising his voice so that most of the people in the bar could hear. The volume of voices decreased discernibly. Two or three people glanced at the doctor's friends and smiled.

'Aye,' the second policeman went on with a smirk, 'but it's no official yet.'

'And they're still after the old one. He'll be caught soon.'

The silence now was static. Everyone stared blankly into their drinks, not knowing whether to denounce the policemen as liars or leave sleeping dogs in peace. Then there was a raucous, drunken laugh from the far side of the bar, by the fire.

'Ye've been had, mate.'

'So "had" they have tae lie,' someone else added.

A third anonymous heckler completed the insult. 'It's pathetic, the state of the force nowadays. Now when I wis a lad . . .'

The rest of his words were drowned in a new burst of babbling all over the room. The policemen, sensing that their prank had gone astray, finished their drinks quickly and left the pub in somewhat unseemly haste.

As the door slammed shut the doctor wiped a bead of sweat from his brow. 'Phew,' he gasped, 'unpleasant pair if ever I saw an unpleasant pair.'

One of the closer-standing drinkers moved to the table and leant down, breathing whisky, until his unshaven face was level with Jim. 'And what will yours be, Jimbo?'

'A whisky'd be great.'

'Two,' said Emma as he turned to her.

'Three,' the doctor put in, even before the man had time to turn to him.

'Good, then doubles it is.'

'Doubles?' The doctor became stern. 'Now wait a minute, these two are sick men.'

'Awww, *c'mon*, doc. Geez a brek, man. This is a celebration.'

The doctor pursed his lips and looked at his two patients who were watching the fracas with amusement. 'Well . . . I s'pose . . .'

'Good.' The unshaven man was away before the doctor could finish his sentence. He reappeared a few minutes later with four double whiskies and a broad grin.

'Cheers!' Jim said, in thanks rather than as a toast, as he took his glass. If it was possible the man's grin widened.

'Thank they polis, no me. It was the fiver they went and left underneath a quick-thinking beer towel as paid for these. Got a mind o' their own, they beer towels.'

Jim and Emma left before dawn the next morning. They were a bit delayed as someone had hidden their trawler in the dry-dock building and had to be woken up to unlock the main doors. The publican, his wife, the doctor and the man who had unlocked the doors, still dressed in his night clothes, said their farewells and waved to them as they left the harbour. In a day someone had done a remarkable amount of work on *Blue Dog*. The bullet holes had been filled up with Pollyfilla, the kitchen cleared up and stocked with more than just the essentials. In the cabin, the publican had left a personal present of three bottles of whisky and six hundred cigarettes. The doctor had left an envelope containing two hundred pounds. This generosity, on top of everything else, deeply touched Jim and Emma. They swore together that, if ever they got the chance, they would pay it all back with interest.

Jim steered out of the loch and into the open sea. It was one of those crisp, crystal-clear winter mornings, the ones that are best enjoyed from inside a snug, warm house. This was the sort of weather the fisherman trusts least. At that time of year, in that part of the world, a fine day is just to lull one into a false sense of security before a really appalling one.

Having reached the wide, grey open sea Jim left the controls and climbed down to the kitchen to make coffee. When he returned to the cabin five minutes later Emma had chopped two lines of coke. She looked at him questioningly.

'Your prescription,' she said, almost tempting him.

Jim grinned. 'Why not?' he said, half to himself. 'Toast, marmalade, coffee and a morphine-cocaine cocktail for breakfast. What more could a man want?' He placed the tray on the table.

'You've taken some of the good doctor's wonder drug?' Emma inquired. Jim nodded, biting off a large corner of toast, piled to gluttonous heights with melted butter and marmalade.

'Perhaps you shouldn't take . . .' Emma began tentatively.

'Don't be silly,' he cut in, his mouth full. Realizing that he had been sharper than he intended he turned, shrugging languidly and added, 'Can't see the harm in it.' He wandered over to the side of the cabin and prodded the newly improvised windows gingerly. 'I'd eat something before you snort, my love,' he said, turning with a slight smile on his face. 'You certainly won't be hungry after a noseful of that stuff.'

Emma grinned. 'Ooh, we do know our stuff, don't we?' she said.

'Never underestimate an Eton man.'

'You were chucked out,' Emma countered, laughing.

'That's what I mean,' he said. 'Before I became a bumpkin, believe it or not, I was an upper-class git.'

'Join the club.'

Jim took a few deep breaths, put the rolled pound note to his right nostril and inhaled one of the lines. He winced, screwing up his nose, and massaged the raped nostril. He returned to the controls.

'How're you feeling now?' Emma inquired, having snorted her line.

'Like I just snorted powdered glass,' he replied. He laughed out loud for the first time in days.

'No, idiot, how's the wound?'

'Omnipresent. How's yours?'

Emma took a swig of the doctor's morphine potion and felt the warm numbness immediately seep into her aching body. It had the peculiar effect of cancelling out most of the outward activity generated by the cocaine whilst hardly affecting her skipping, leaping mind. It was, she thought, a feeling of extreme wellbeing.

'How's the wound?' Jim repeated.

'Hurts.'

Emma looked up after a bit, having had no response from Jim, to find him watching their starboard quarter through binoculars.

'Sea-pigs,' he announced. 'Try the radio.' 'Unidentified trawler to police launches, over. Do you read me?' she said.

'We read you loud and clear,' the police launch said back. Jim took over the radio.

'Good,' he said deliberately. 'Then you can hear me telling you to go fuck yourselves. Over and out.'

For a while their two courses converged. But *Blue Dog*, as Jim had guessed, had the edge. When they were only half a mile or so apart, Jim pulled out the throttle and the two police launches were forced to pull in behind as their prey outran them.

'See how this mother shifts,' Jim remarked proudly as they pulled away. The followers accelerated, giving chase right across the Minch. But *Blue Dog* could keep them at a safe distance, cruising whilst they pushed their smaller craft as fast as they would go. After two hours they reached the coast of Harris. Jim turned south, keeping Harris a mile to the right. After another few minutes they cruised past Renish Point and into the Sound of Harris; the police boats were still doggedly following. *Blue Dog* swerved in between the tiny islands of Langay and Gilsay, cut in behind Groay, circled its south coast and turned back towards Harris. Jim held this course for exactly five minutes before turning ninety degrees towards the Sound of Berneray. He steered around the sandbanks which point south-east in a long spit from Berneray and halted behind them. The police thought they had him. They altered course from the safe route around the submerged sandbank, which Jim had just taken, and headed straight for him. Five minutes later the foremost of the launches was hopelessly grounded. The second veered away, suddenly realizing Jim's ploy. But by that time *Blue Dog* was heading for the Sound of Berneray. The remaining police boat tried to follow him through it, beyond Boreray and into the open Atlantic.

The boats bucked and heaved as the redoubled Atlantic surge struck them. Jim made a quick educated guess and kept on out to sea. As he had hoped the police boat soon banked away and turned back to help its friend, defeated by the power of the seas.

It was now two o'clock and Jim was both tired and bored. He gave the controls to Emma and retired to the table to smoke and relax. She held the boat out into the ocean for a few more miles before turning south. Jim radioed Pirate to tell them where he was and why. When he was asked where they were headed he answered by humming a few bars of a local lullaby called 'Mingulay'. This pretty song is about one of the two southernmost islands of the outer Hebrides. With its brother island, Berneray (not to be confused with the Berneray at the other end of Uist), it lies off Barra and is about as far west as one can get in Britain proper. Barring St Kilda, sixty miles west of Lewis, there are no more remote places in the Western Isles. Few people would know of Mingulay's existence, fewer still would ever have heard the lullaby. But the fishermen would, and they were the ones who mattered.

They gave Barra a wide berth and chugged on to Mingulay. It was dusk by this time, the pole star just beginning to twinkle above the northern horizon. The sun was sinking, a deep red ball, sending shards of crimson light into the western sky, which deepened to a deep blue over the Hebrides and faded to black over the mainland. The sun slid into the sea with a last, spectacular flourish. It was a wonderfully beautiful swan song for the winter day. A path of sparkling orange spread across the massive ocean like a highway to infinity. Cliffs towered over their heads, dark, jagged buttresses glistening and glittering, a wall of uncut jet. And above, behind, in front, all around, thousand upon thousand of sea birds, taking the last shelter before the wild, open sea, wheeled and soared, making a deafening noise.

Some dipped and dived into the wash caused by the small trawler, appearing with wriggling fish clamped in their beaks. Gannets circled further away and dropped like white thunderbolts into the sea. The rest contented themselves by having a last fly and a final meal before the onset of the blisteringly cold night – the herring gulls, high in the updrafts which rose off the cliffs; the fulmars, soaring around with their long, tapering wings outstretched, unbeating, just as their larger cousins, the albatrosses, glide across whole oceans without ever beating their great wings. The puffins and auks too made an appearance, dipping over the waves, the puffins' multi-coloured beaks catching the dying sun. All of these and many, many more played in the rapidly dimming light. Ducks, geese, waders, divers and even the occasional falcon were all out in the air around Mingulay.

Jim contemplated the wild freedom of the small island with its massive colonies of birds, untouched and, for the most part, unseen by mankind. He had always yearned for that kind of solitude, far away from humanity, cares, laws. In moments of daydreaming he had wished that he was an animal or a bird, and now, the irony of it, he was being hunted like one. The feeling that this was the perfect paradise so obliterated anything else, as he guided *Blue Dog* through to the twilit side of Mingulay, that the sight which met his eyes on the eastern side of the island caught him completely off guard. He gasped.

'Fuck me,' he said, awestruck.

'What is it?' Emma asked from the steep staircase which she was trying to negotiate with a large tray.

'Come and look.'

She obeyed, and looked in the direction Jim was pointing.

'Jesus Christ.'

There were perhaps thirty big Arctic trawlers, a sight rarely seen in the Western Isles, let alone here.

'What the hell are *they* doing here?' Emma said, her voice full of amazement.

'I didn't know there were any fishing fleets left,' Jim replied, hushed with awe.

At that moment the intercom crackled and they heard a thick Yorkshire accent: 'Ullo? Ullo? You *Blue Dog?*'

'Yes', Emma radioed back.

'Di you read uz?'

'Loud and clear.'

'Dead ace.' There was a shout at the far end, as if the original speaker was calling someone to the intercom. A new voice came on to the line, again with a strong Yorkshire accent.

'OK, *Blue Dog*, let's quit the cackle. Thought it'd be you, we did. We're going to 'Ull so you'd best stick with uz.'

'Sorry?' Emma asked, baffled.

'Sound bloody dozey ter me,' the Yorkshireman said over his shoulder. He turned back to the intercom.

'We're going ter 'Ull and yer'd best stick with uz. There's enoof sea-pigs 'round 'ere ter swamp yer.'

'Fine . . . Would it be stupid to ask what you're doing in the Hebrides?' Emma asked. There was a laugh somewhere behind the man on the far end of the line. He snorted.

'Nope. We're doing the same as you, son. We've joost run 'alf way 'cross the North Atlantic with 'alf the bloody Icelandic Navy on our tail.'

The person behind him laughed again.

84

'Full brownie points for starting a new cod war.'

'Bugger off, Dunstan, yer great prat,' the speaker said away from the mouthpiece. Then, back to the radio:

'Sorry, son. Just get your bum in 'ere with uz and not a pig in the world'll get near yer.'

'Cheers,' Emma replied and hung up. She slowly turned to Jim, grinning.

'Hull?' He sounded dumbfounded.

'Bad news travels fast.'

'Jesus, Hull, though? We'll be on to Fleet Street next.'

On the way north, back up the Minch, the fleet of trawlers saw six police launches, travelling south in convoy. The intercom crackled with taunts and barely veiled insults from the Yorkshiremen.

'Well if it isn't the boys in blue. What brings them 'ere at this time of night?' one voice said.

'Long past their bedtime, it is,' someone else added.

'Pissy little boats, they 'ave. Mind yer don't capsize in wer wash, copper.'

'I 'erd,' remarked the voice that belonged to the man called Dunstan.

'I 'erd that a pig got itself grounded earlier on.' Gales of raucous laughter followed this observation. The police ignored it and steamed away southwards.

At midnight Jim gave the controls to Emma and climbed downstairs to catch up on lost sleep. He slept through their brief pit-stop in Benbecula and was still alseep long after dawn had broken, revealing heavy, ominous clouds to the north-east. They left the Minch, with Lewis gradually disappearing astern, and rounded Cape Wrath. It occurred to Emma that they were taking an inexplicably long route back to Hull, but she did not complain. It was then half-past ten in the morning and Jim finally surfaced, looking and feeling rested and better than he had been for some time. By now the sea had become rough and the clouds were closing in fast.

Jim appeared through the hatch, wearing fresh jeans and a clean tee-shirt bearing the faded words Official Moby Maclean Fan Club. He was holding two cups of coffee.

'Where are we?'

Emma acknowledged his presence with a tired smile, not moving from her seat. 'The wrong side of Cape Wrath.'

'You what? What on earth are we doing here?'

'Seemed like a good idea, I guess.'

Jim walked across the cabin to Emma, squaring his legs against the pitching of the boat. He kissed her gently on the back of the neck. She turned around, murmuring 'More.' Jim smiled and kissed her on the forehead, then on the lips. They held together for a while, embracing tightly. It was Jim who broke away, planting a small kiss on her cheek.

'Get some sleep, my love. You've been up here for hours.'

Emma yawned and stood up. She faced him, smiling warily. 'We can't go on like this for ever, Jim.'

'I'm working on it, babe.'

When Emma had gone to bed Jim turned his mind to the question she had just asked. How long could they go on like this, had been her meaning. They could not go on and on running indefinitely. Emma seemed to be relatively hale, but how long would that continue? She had suffered a bad wound and was likely to grow steadily weaker as the days went by. Jim was worried. His mind fought back and forwards between conflicting thoughts and emotions. The most attractive idea was to postpone any decision until some later date. But procrastination would not make matters any better. And besides, procrastination implies that there will be a tomorrow to stall until. Jim could not be sure what the next hour would bring, let alone the next day.

Hour after hour he racked his brains for a solution to his dilemma. The only thing that occurred to him, in a blinding flash of realization, was that he alone was guilty of a particular crime. He had fired the fatal shots, he had stolen the boat and he was mainly at fault when it came to the stealing and subsequent withholding of the cocaine. When the trouble came to a head, as it surely would, then his actions would come down on two innocent people like a ton of lead. The mere fact that it had taken five days for him to see this simple thing shocked Jim immensely. In this quarter, at least, he could clear up a few loose ends. He fetched a pen and some paper, returned to the controls, and tried to compose a confession.

Twenty cigarettes later, after four hours of writing, scrapping, writing more and throwing away still more he had written a rough draft. The bin was full of paper, crumpled into loose balls, the ashtray was overflowing. It was not so much a lack of the necessary bravery which confounded his efforts, it was rather a sort of pride in the best and most chivalrous way to do it. The object was not only to take the blame, but to take it with style and panache.

The weather grew progressively worse as they moved eastwards. If it had not been for the fleet, Jim found himself thinking, *Blue Dog* could not possibly have stood up to such a hurricane. But then, if it had not been for the Yorkshiremen *Blue Dog* would not have been near such an infamous part of the world in the first place. As it was, with the big trawlers all around closed in to within fifty feet on every side, the waves broke over them and landed on *Blue Dog* with such ferocity that Jim thought his frail craft might sink at any moment.

In the end he was forced to shout to Emma. Although the pumps were working overtime they were not enough to drain the deck. The boat was creaking and shuddering under the thunderous waves. Someone had to unclog the scuppers and bale a ton of water off the deck, or *Blue Dog* would not survive. He radioed to the fleet and warned them what he was going to do, asking for as much cover as they could give. Even the bluff Yorkshiremen seemed worried and nervous. The stretch of water between Cape Wrath and the Pentland Firth, south of Orkney, had been known to sink far bigger boats than these and this was not a normal storm, even by the appalling standards set by this area. It took as much gas to keep the boats away from the rugged cliffs, but close enough for them to provide some shield against the worst of the waves, as it took to actually move forwards. The currents were tricky even without the storm. But the weather report from London told of force nine gales; and they were giving a liberal estimate from six hundred miles away. Out in the centre of it the gusts were blowing right up to force twelve and more, hurricane force.

The fleet moved in even closer to *Blue Dog*, hugging the rugged, treacherous cliffs. By doing this they kept to slightly calmer seas as the waves fell back on themselves, thundering back off the coast and lessening the mountainous impact of the waves that rode in. But the currents dragged in every direction, causing whirlpools and pulling violently, hauling the rudders off course constantly.

Emma took the wheel while Jim first tied a long rope to the cooker downstairs, then attached the other end to a harness he wore like a waistcoat. He put on a lifejacket over the whole affair and reversed out on to the deck, feeding the rope through his hands as he moved backwards. The door, hampered by the rope, slammed almost shut, then swung open, as each new gust caught it, light as an autumn leaf in the gale.

Out on deck the effect of the combined elements made attempts to remain upright akin to standing in a wind

tunnel, being blasted from every side by fire hoses. Jim slid
to and fro, grabbing handfuls of dirt, seaweed, fish and
other assorted rubbish from the scuppers. In the end,
giving up the exhausting task of trying to stay on his feet
he took to sliding around on his belly. The task took a
great deal of time and effort, but one by one he emptied
the scuppers and the water flowed through, raising *Blue
Dog* inches in the sea.

Meanwhile he was missing a vicious argument which
was being hurled this way and that over the intercom. It
was not difficult for Emma to understand what was being
said, although she was not meant to, as the fight was over
Blue Dog. The arguers spoke in jargon and insults. The
problem, as Emma understood it, lay with a Scottish
captain in the fleet. There were eight trawlers surrounding
Blue Dog and another twenty-four lying in a wider arc
stretching from a mile in front in a curve away from the
cliffs, back to a mile behind.

The three boats which lay on the inside of *Blue Dog*,
nearest the cliffs, were under the direct command of the
Yorkshiremen. They had by far the most dangerous job
but they were all friends of the lead captain – Skipper. He
obviously trusted them and they, in turn, obeyed and
trusted him unquestioningly. Behind *Blue Dog* there was a
group of trawlers led by another independent Humberman, and the full ferocity of the gale landed on them.
Despite this broadside from the elements and despite the
fact that there was not a great deal of love lost between
the two Yorkshiremen, they remained loyal. But in front
there were four trawlers led by a sarcastic and bolshie Scot.
It was he who caused the fight. His boats were acting as
a buffer, arranged in a V directly in front of *Blue Dog*, to
cut away the worst of the waves which rode down the line
of the coast. He was, it has to be said, performing an
extremely difficult and unpleasant task. At first he radioed

89

Skipper, saying that he wanted to lie further out to sea, well away from the cliffs. Then that they should spread out more so that more boats could share the load he was bearing alone. When Skipper answered that this would seriously endanger *Blue Dog*, there was a dry laugh.

'I couldn't give a tuppeny fuck for *Blue* frigging *Dog*,' came his answer. 'Leave the bugger. She's a liability.' This irritated Skipper no end. The argument waxed to a slanging match in which the expletives and insults had Emma wincing. At last the Scotsman suggested turning back. Again Skipper fought this idea tooth and nail. The Scotsman began to concede defeat and Skipper, accordingly, pushed his advantage. Ten minutes later the four front trawlers broke rank and wheeled away back towards Cape Wrath.

Jim was standing when he saw the dim shapes turn. For a moment he did not realize what was happening and just muttered to himself that it was odd. He watched the boats disappear into the driving rain, his mind registering nothing but mild puzzlement, then he suddenly looked very afraid and turned to run back to the cabin. He knew, in that split second, that any change in the path of the front boats would have a devastating effect on anyone behind. He was right, but not fast enough to celebrate about it. The combination of the washes thrown by the turning trawlers and the enormous strength of the unfettered sea was terrifying. Eight waves hit *Blue Dog* in quick succession, hurling it this way and that. Then the main waves, for the previous eight were just the washes, struck. *Blue Dog* bucked around like a toy. The anxious watchers saw their small, frail friend being thrown over the crest of each new wave, then dropping with sickening crashes into the troughs. Once, the small boat came within feet of capsizing. It landed in a trough facing slightly off the line of the next wave. Emma had no time to right it before the hill of water

90

curled high over the cabin. For a moment the whole boat was submerged as tons of water exploded over it. Then it bobbed clear again.

By a miracle *Blue Dog* survived the first wave, came clear of the second, weathered the next two and beat four more. It was under five minutes before the Yorkshiremen to the north had filled the gap. But in that time Jim was very nearly killed. He was tossed about like a puppet worked by a mad puppetmaster. He was picked up, smashed against the deck, the cabin, the sides . . . everything. He was crushed on to the deck by a deluge and, at last, thrown overboard.

For a second he was under water, sinking. Then the lifejacket did its job and he shot to the surface, paralysed with cold. He gasped for air, yelling out in agony and fear. Then he reached out a hand and began to drag himself up the rope. Emma saw it suddenly go taut across the cabin. Then it went slack, taut again, slack and taut, slack, taut, slack, taut as Jim heaved it in foot by foot. He felt, suddenly, that he was going to die. The extreme cold, the sheer effort of pulling himself into a boat travelling at speed in tempestuous seas almost beat him. These combined to take him to the threshold of giving up and allowing the sea to take him into its bosom. A remark of Ian's rang wildly in his head, echoing back and forwards, sometimes quiet, sometimes in a shout: 'Three minutes, at most, before you die of exposure.'

The words galvanized him. 'Can't die,' he gasped and began to pull the rope with renewed, frenzied vigour. Emma watched, transfixed as the second attack pulled the rope as tight as a guitar string. She could not leave the controls, she could not help . . . just watch. Jim pulled himself up to the side of the boat and, with a final stupendous dip into his rapidly diminishing resources, got himself over the side on to the deck. There he lay, exhausted,

91

vomiting sea water in great, tearing retches. He crawled like an injured animal into the cabin, pulling in the rope behind him and dragging the door closed. Then he slumped half-dead on the floor.

'Jim?' Emma said from the wheel.

Her voice rose to a scream: 'Jim?' He turned over, blood dribbling from the side of his mouth. Emma stared, horrified, then left the controls. She manhandled him into a sitting position, avoiding a spurt of vomit. With expert speed she tore off his lifejacket and harness. Already the water was freezing on his sweater. She pulled it off and threw it over her shoulder. His chest was stained with blood and the stitches put in by the doctor had torn out, opening his wound again. As he began to come round she tore off his jeans. The skin all over his body was blotchy, in places bluish. He was covered with bruises and cuts.

Emma left him for a moment and ran for one of the bottles of whisky left on the boat by the Ullapool landlord. Jim drank it in huge gulps, dribbling a great deal from the corners of his mouth. He coughed violently, vomited again, then took the bottle in shaking hands and drank some more.

'What the fuck're you up to, *Blue Dog*?' Skipper's voice came over the radio. Emma stood up, seeing for the first time that the current had carried them to within a stone's throw of the boats between *Blue Dog* and the shore, forcing them even nearer to the cliffs. She grabbed the controls, then picked up the intercom and apologized.

'How's your friend?' Skipper asked.

'Alive.'

'Then he'll live.'

Emma stayed at the controls and left Jim to recover with the whisky. The gale began to abate slightly but the currents became worse. The fleet steered away from the cliffs.

92

After some time, two hours since Jim had nearly drowned, the intercom crackled into life.

'If I'm right,' the Yorkshireman said unsurely, 'Thurso and Scrabster are in the next bay. We're stopping there the night. Orkney's another hour north but I'd advise you not to try the Pentland on yer tod.'

'Fine. Then I'm with you.'

'Good-o. I feel like getting meself pissed, I do.'

They swerved into Thurso Bay. The lights of the town twinkled up ahead. They had made it.

One by one the trawlers limped into Thurso harbour and docked. Emma hid *Blue Dog* between two of the biggest ones and disembarked, supporting Jim. They were met by Skipper on the jetty. He was a big man, six feet four of muscle and joviality. He had a bushy, greying beard which partially concealed a long scar that crossed his left cheekbone in a jagged white line. He wore a tea-cosy hat, pulled well down over his brows, and blue overalls. After greeting Jim and Emma loudly and pumping their hands up and down he grinned like a wolf.

'Thought yer'd 'ad it there, we did.'

'Same here,' replied Emma, noticing how very upperclass her accent was beside this born and bred Humberman.

'Let's get some booze inside of us.' He shouted down the pier and led the group that gathered around in search of a pub. After a few minutes they invaded a sleazy-looking bar on the harbour, noisily shouting for whisky and rum. They sat down – Jim, Emma, Skipper and two other tough little Yorkshiremen around a table. The others crowded the bar.

For a while they chatted about the journey, Jim and Emma keeping quiet as the conversation invariably returned to the Scotsman who had deserted. He was described variously as a coward, a bastard, an idiot, a self-centred moron and a few other foul terms. There was a strong element of anger and contempt, as if this were just the latest in a long line of arguments with him. This was proved when Skipper pointed to his scar.

'See this? That bastard of a muther-fooking Scots coward gave uz that. Did it with a bloody kitchen knife, the little rat.' Neither Jim nor Emma knew how to react to this. They looked at each other.

'Shit,' said Jim.

'I got 'im though,' Skipper added with relish, 'cracked him over the nut with a soda syphon ... Ever heard a skull break?' They admitted that they were yet to have that pleasure. 'Nasty, it is, sort of splat.' And so on.

After a while his two companions pushed away through the crowd to buy more drink. Skipper watched them go before turning quickly to Emma.

'How come you go 'round pretending to be a man?'

Emma coloured slightly. 'What d'you mean?'

'Well, you're a bird.'

'Why d'you think that?'

One of his two companions had sneaked back with a bottle of whisky and sat down, laughing raucously.

'Bloody voi-err watched yer snogging through 'is binocs.'

Skipper cuffed him with his bear-like hand. 'Piss off, Dunstan, yer little sneak.'

The man laughed even louder, leaning back in his chair and feebly fending off more blows with his arms.

''E turns 'round ...' Dunstan stopped, overcome by a new bout of laughter. ' ... 'E turns 'round, 'is face all shocked, like, and 'e says ter me, he says, "Yer know them two blokes on that trawler. Well they're kissing each other." ' Again Dunstan dissolved into fits of merry laughter.

'And I takes the binocs and 'as a peek an' turns to 'im ...' He gesticulated towards Skipper, trying to assume

94

a straight face. ' "Skipper," I says, "that's no bloke," I says. "'Ow come?" he says . . . "Ave yer ever seen a bloke fondling another bloke's tit?" I answers.' Tears rolled down Dunstan's cheeks and he groaned. 'Fook me', he succeeded in gasping at last.

The other man nodded towards Skipper, looking at Emma. 'You'll 'ave ter excuse wer Skipper,' he said. "E'll remember that till 'e dies, 'e will. 'Asn't seen any sex in ten years, 'as Bill.'

So began another round of mobbing big Skipper. Him insulting and hitting for all his worth, the other two helpless with laughter.

The next morning brought calmer weather. The fishermen had left shortly after dawn. Most of them had not been to bed, taking full advantage of the flexible licensing hours in Scotland and getting themselves smashed before braving the fierce North Sea. They made such a noise, singing and shouting drunken abuse at each other, that the police had to be called in to get rid of them.

Emma and Jim saw them off, thanking Skipper heartily and ordering him to come and see them in Argyll if they ever came out of this affair alive and free. The Yorkshiremen stared down at them for almost a minute before answering.

'You take care of yourselves . . . Yer stupid Scotch bastards.' He was not capable of keeping up the heartfelt farewell without suffixing it with a light insult. But they both respected that inability and thanked him again, assuring him that they did not intend to do anything he would not do. This made him laugh uproariously. He shook his head and yelled over his shoulder.

'Take uz away from these Scotch prats, Dunstan, afore they get uz into trouble.'

After they had gone the two fugitives had a large break-

fast. Emma finished first and walked to the boat. After she had gone Jim pushed away the remains of his food and left the café in a hurry. He ran to a newsagent first and bought a newspaper, shielding his face in shadow behind an upraised hand in case, by some misfortune, his mug shot was in it. Then he sprinted to a post office where he bought a first-class stamp, stuck it to an envelope he had produced from a pocket and walked outside. For a minute of indecision he wavered, holding the letter at the mouth of the letter box, then he laughed to himself, muttering, 'Coward'. The thought seemed to give him new resolve. He looked at the envelope, a last sad, wry glance. Then he slipped it into the letter box and made his way back to *Blue Dog*.

'Let his epitaph be,' he said out loud, 'the fire that burned his boats, cooked his goose.' Then a smile grew on his face, as if he suddenly felt lightheaded, with such a weight off his mind. He laughed out loud, amazing an old lady who was wobbling along the kerb, using her stick more as an aggressive weapon against any opposition in her path than as a support.

Rob Roy

When Ian left Loch Nevis he easily shook off the police behind Soay Island and immediately doubled back to Oban. A day after he had parted with *Blue Dog* he sighted the weird little acropolis which presides over the thriving fishing town of Oban. This was not Mallaig, stuck away on the northern point of the Western Isles fishing grounds; nor Ullapool, even further north but slightly larger than Mallaig. In a peculiar, localized sense Oban deserves its droll, somewhat bizarre acropolis. As the fulcrum, terminal and base for everyone who owes their living to this corner of the earth it holds a position of great importance, especially for people who have never seen a bigger town.

Ian was not the sort of person who thought twice about taking risks. He knew that Oban would be crawling with policemen and he also knew exactly what the police would be thinking. The last place in the entire archipelago that they would expect either *Rob Roy* or Blue Dog to be was actually in Oban. It was almost worth the risk of being caught just to stop in and make fools of them right under their noses. He took his boat up the Firth of Lorn and hid it in a small bay on an island called Eilean Dubh, between Lismore and Benderloch, in the Lynn of Lorn. It was mid-afternoon and it was raining. Lismore rose out of the firth like the back of a huge whale, obscured by curtains of rain. Without thinking twice Ian left *Rob Roy* and rowed to the mainland, walked a little way to a road and hitched a lift back to Oban.

By the time he had reached the town it was pelting. He thanked the butcher heartily for giving him a lift, glad to be away from the overpowering smell of raw meat, and trotted to the nearest pub. He entered in a rush, tearing off his overcoat as he ordered a pint from the door. In answer the barman gave him a look that would have reduced most people to a pile of dust. In one rapid eye exchange the man succeeded in conveying a mixture of hunted terror, loathing and warning. Without hesitation Ian knew what that look meant. He glanced around the room and saw three policemen sitting in the corner. Luckily they were deeply engrossed in conversation and had not yet looked up to pass the customary greetings with the newcomer. They were all men that Ian knew by name and there was no doubt that they knew him.

In a surprisingly casual movement Ian was across to the far side of the bar, out of view. The barman caught his arm and hustled him into a back room. It smelt acrid and unpleasant, stale cigarettes and sweat mingling to impart a general aura of dirt and lack of hygiene. The room seemed to be kitchen, living room and playroom for the proprietor and his family. In one corner the wife sat, a purple-haired, ugly battle-axe of a woman clad in a greasy apron and cheap, dirty clothes. She was reading the *Sun*, a cigarette hanging out of her mouth. The ash was longer than what remained of the cigarette itself but, judging by the filthy state of the carpet, this was a minor problem.

Ian took all of this in as he came through the door. He was vaguely disgusted and the smell assaulted his nostrils, but he was not particularly perturbed.

'Whit in hell're you daeing here, ye great eejit?' the barman demanded in a hoarse whisper. His wife looked up, acknowledged their presence with a nod and went back to her paper, ignoring the ash that had dropped on to her lap.

'I need a hand,' Ian replied quietly.

The barman did a very convincing mime of angry exasperation. 'You sail richt into Oban to tell me that?' The softness of his accent somehow made the rebuke far more vicious.

'Aye. I need a hand,' Ian repeated.

'Christ. Take what ye need and scarper out o' my pub. Chust get out o' my pub, will ye.'

'When I said I needed a hand I meant just that. I'm gonnae run the islands and I'm no gonnae be able tae dae it on ma ain.'

'Where's yer Lord and his preety cousin, then?' the man jeered.

Ian shook his head, and his voice betrayed an edge of the anger which was boiling up inside him: 'Mind yer mouth, Callagan, or I'll pit yer teeth doon yer throat.'

'Well, where are they?'

'Can ye no read the papers, ye stupid bastard? Jim killed a man yesterday . . . He's running.'

'Oh, bloody clever that wass. Mind you they MacGregors have allus been a stupid, murderous lot. Auld Nick's bluid in 'em.'

Ian glared at Callagan, narrowing his eyes with undisguised contempt. For a moment he contemplated pummelling the foolish, smug smile off his face. But the urge quickly passed.

'Yer husband's a prick, Missus Callagan,' he remarked, still glowering at the barman.

The woman looked up. 'Aye, I ken fine.'

'And a coward.'

'I ken fine.'

After a moment Ian shrugged and turned away. He walked to the back door and opened it.

'I'll mind ye for yer help, Callagan,' he flung acidly over his shoulder, and slammed the door. The barman stared at it, his face contorted with hatred. Then his wife stood up, absentmindedly flicking more ash on the floor.

'It's no as if yer no the most unpopular man in Oban anyway,' she remarked.

'Shut yer face, woman,' her husband snapped. Then he returned to the bar, an evil look in his eye.

One by one Ian tried every pub he knew in his search for a companion. The reception he got in some of them was nervous and fretful. To even be known to have harboured Ian MacGillavray for a few minutes put their livelihoods in jeopardy. Others were hospitable and kind. Ian was offered more rifles, supplies, drink and advice than he could possibly cope with, but no one wanted to go with him.

As last he stumbled into a pub at the top end of town. It was nearly midnight and Ian was soaked, tired and maudlin. He had been drinking all evening and was rapidly losing his faith in Oban. To make matters worse the local radio had heard little from or about Jim. Even in the light of day, stone-cold sober, Ian had doubted Jim's ability to navigate the islands without help, and Emma's stamina to stand up to such a long stretch at sea. And, from what he had seen during their brief meeting on Loch Nevis, neither of them was in exactly the best condition to subject themselves to an indefinite chase around the Western Isles. He had been able to push the thought from his mind then, but now it returned in renewed strength and torpedoed all of the arguments which had convinced him earlier on.

There were five silent drinkers in the pub. The barman was leaning on the bar in a way that suggested he had had enough, emotionally as well as physically, for one day. The barmaid – a girl who would have seemed like a candidate for a lemonade shandy and a Mars bar, if it was not for a very well-formed frontage – was apathetically cleaning mugs. She would twirl a damp towel around the inside of each glass for minutes on end and then place the mugs on the bar with a quarter of an inch of soapy water in the bottom. Someone had a brief try on the slot machine, lost thirty pence and gave up, partly through drunken lethargy and partly because of the disapproving looks everyone else gave him. The barman opened one eye, livid with crimson veins, and studied the offender with distaste before allowing the eyelid to slip gently back into its former position.

The door burst open and a youth sprinted in, gasping for breath. 'Whar's the auld man? . . . Ian MacGillavray?' he panted out.

One of the less comatose people at the bar looked at Ian, then at the boy. 'Wheesht, lad. Whit's the hurry?'

'They polis. They're aifter 'im.'

Suddenly everyone was awake and staring at him. Ian was out of his seat and over to the door in a flash.

'How d'you ken, Callum?' the barmaid inquired, smiling reassuringly. She was pretty when she smiled, with dimples on her red cheeks and big, kind eyes.

Callum, who seemed to be somewhat overawed by the attention he had drawn to himself, smiled shyly back at the girl, recognizing her as a friend. 'I've bin all over toon, Mairy. Yon bas . . . Callagan went and sneaked tae the polis. They're searching every pub in Oban.'

The barman laughed at this. 'They ken their man, then. Eh, Ian?'

The boy swung around, realizing for the first time that Ian was just behind him. He blushed right down to the roots of his curly red hair.

'Sorr . . . sorry, Mister MacGillavray.' He spun back to the barmaid, confused in his hurry, 'But they're up tae the Red Lion so they've only got thon posh hotel afore they're here.'

101

Ian glanced nervously out of the door. The barman swore under his breath. 'Quick, Ian,' he said, 'out the back. Callum'll show ye the way.'

Callum took Ian by the arm and pulled him to the back door. It was pitch-dark outside. They ran through the outdoor urinals, both unconsciously holding their breaths against the foul, bitter smell. Then they were into the back yard. It was surrounded by a high wooden fence.

'Ye'll no be expecting me tae climb that?' Ian asked with a smile.

The boy laughed, shaking his head, and hurled himself against it. Three upright slats gave way, pivoting to a horizontal position in the middle. Both people dived through and Callum closed his escape route, still grinning all over his almost attractively ugly, freckled face.

'It'll take 'em 'oors tae find thon,' he boasted. Then he grabbed Ian's arm again and led him away from the pub. By way of a series of shortcuts, through gardens, back streets and car parks, they crossed the entire town without touching a main road for more than ten or twenty yards. As they ran, the youth politely but nervously kept himself from completely outrunning Ian, who was puffing away, always a few yards behind. Ian breathlessly asked him what he was doing out so late at night.

'Looking fer you!' came the swift reply, which was fair enough. Realizing that his answer had been a bit curt he added, 'A'hm allus up late. I help they fishermen when they come in.'

'Does yer mum no mind?' the obvious question.

'Ma mum's deid. Sae's ma dad.' Ian was caught off balance by the answer to his humdrum question. It shocked him deeply that a child could be so matter of fact, even blasé, about such a traumatic thing. The boy must have been an orphan for a very long time to behave as if there were no grief, no regrets inside him for the parents he had lost.

At last they reached the harbour. They slunk down the road, avoiding the street lights where they could. They came to an alley and Callum ducked into it, almost losing Ian as he suddenly disappeared. Ian ran in behind him.

'Wait here, Mister MacGillavray. A'hm goan fir the moped.'

Ian swore to himself, wondering whether a tactical retreat on a moped was worth the discomfort and indignity. A moment later Callum reappeared from the back of the cul de sac wheeling a machine that, by no stretch of the imagination, was a moped. It was the biggest and quickest bike a learner driver is allowed to take on the roads, a monster to Ian's eye. It was metallic blue and gave the impression of being considerably larger and more powerful than it actually was. On the back was a black metal box; Ian was supposed to perch in between this and Callum. His young escort, obviously at home on this evil-looking beast, threw Ian a helmet and put on his own.

'Where d'you get the cash fer this?' Ian asked as he gingerly straddled the bike.

The youth gave him a quick, appraising look and appeared to come to a spot decision. 'Ah nicked it afore ah left Glesgae.' With that he mounted the machine and kick-started it, revving the shuddering engine into life. He turned and his voice, muffled by the helmet, rose above the growling of the engine.

'Where to, Sur?'

'Up the loch, ye ken Barcaldine Castle, the ither side o' Connel?'

'Aye, ah do that.'

'Just there would dae fine.'

'Okey-doke.' With that Callum let his hand off the clutch and the bike bucked forwards, banked left and sped off down the jetty. Ian shut his eyes, held on for dear life and pretended that this was not happening.

Contrary to his appearance Callum was not a fool. Most people would have raced to get clear of Oban if they were with Ian. But Callum knew that this would be idiotic and stuck rigidly to thirty miles an hour. They passed five police cars before they reached the edge of town; one sat beside them, an arm's length away, at a traffic light. But the boy did not flinch or hesitate; he kept his cool until he was out on to the darkened road. Then he accelerated through three gears and leapt forward up the tree-lined shore of the Firth of Lorn.

It took half an hour to reach the spot where Ian had landed. After Connel, when the bright street lights glowed red through his eyelids, Ian opened his eyes again. He leant over Callum's neck, making it quite clear that he was searching for the correct turning off the road, so further haste was unnecessary. He recognized the concealed entrance to the track which led to Barcaldine Castle and tapped the youth on the shoulder. Callum slammed the bike down through the gears, making the engine scream and the tyres skid. He drifted around the corner and accelerated off the main road. A minute later Ian again indicated to the right and they turned on to an even smaller track. On a third indication from his passenger Callum slipped the engine into neutral, they glided to a halt and both dismounted. Callum wheeled it into the trees and produced a carefully folded length of tarpaulin from the case on the back.

'Whit're ye daeing?' Ian inquired.

'Covering ma bike, or it'll get rusty.'

'Why, though?'

The boy looked up, slightly surprised, and shrugged. 'Cos if water gets on the metal it . . .'

'Ye cannae come wi' me,' Ian butted in.

'Why no? Ah can lift as much as any yin. A'hm eighteen and there's nae yin tae miss me.'

'But I'm wanted . . . By the polis.'

The dramatic emphasis Ian put into the last three words was lost on the youth. He shrugged his shoulders nonchalantly. 'Same here.'

' . . . And I'm no taking passengers.'

'A'hm no esking yez tae take on passengers.'

'Ye could get hurt, or chucked in the Borstal.'

'So? It wouldnae be the first time.'

All the while he was covering up his bike; lying it on its side, smothering it with the tarpaulin, then scattering branches, leaves and dirt over that. He finished and stood up, looking proudly at his handiwork. In the dark not a square inch of either bike or tarpaulin was visible. Callum turned to Ian.

'Come on, Mister MacGillavray. They'll hiv us sussed by now.'

'Ye'll be missed,' Ian attempted, somewhat feebly. So far his arguments had been parried expertly. Callum seemed to be prepared for any eventuality.

'Ah telt Mister McLuskey a'hd go with yez if ye'd let us. He'll tell every yin else.'

'Who's Mister McLuskey?' Ian asked.

The boy gave him a look of mixed amazement and pity. 'Him o' the Red Lion.'

For a few seconds they stared at each other. Then Ian in turn shrugged, pulling down the corners of his mouth.

'What the hell,' he said out loud, and began to make his way to the shore. Callum followed. Together they found the rowboat and, one at each oar, pulled away from the shore. Their conversation continuing right out to where *Rob Roy* lay – curt, monosyllabic sentences on one side, quiet replies on the other.

'Ye'll no complain!' An order rather than a question.

'No.'

'Ye'll dae whit yer told.'

'Aye.'

'Ye'll no nick anything.'

'Would I?'

'Would you?'

'No.'

'Promise?'

'Promise.'

A brief pause, broken only by the slapping of the oars against the water and the screech of an owl away over on Lismore.

'Ye'll make ma coffee.'

A small laugh. 'Aye.'

Another brief silence, then a snort of laughter from Ian.

'If yer lying . . .'

'I'm no.' The protest was in a strident, offended whine, carrying well across the water and echoing slightly in the crisp night air.

'Shush, will yez?' Ian hissed. 'They'll hear ye frae Mull.'

'Sorry.'

'And no whining.'

A tired sigh. 'No.'

'No slacking.'

'*No, no, no, no* . . . C'mon mun, geez a brek.'

'Ye'll call me sir.'

'Aye, fine, OK, sure . . . geez a brek, *sur*.' Then muffled laughter.

'Ye cheeky wee bastard,' Ian remarked accusingly.

'Aye, ah am that . . . sur.'

And so on, all the way to the boat.

In the next few days Ian's initial reaction to the boy altered greatly. He ceased to be irritated by Callum's constant quips which came back, fast as light, on the tail of every command. He was a tough, wiry little Glaswegian with a streak of animal cunning and a great deal of street wisdom.

106

He was also determined to prove himself. He spent the first day scrubbing, washing, tidying, polishing and doing his utmost to please Ian. To a great extent he succeeded.

On the second day, which was rough, he spent nine hours throwing up over the side. But by the third day he had overcome his nausea and was into the swing of things. He had already worked out how a trawler operated, having a quick, as well as mechanical, mind. He enjoyed doing menial chores that Ian, or Jim, or indeed Emma were far too exalted to lower themselves to without first putting up a good fight. In all he was a bright, eager, shy child. The better half of rough urban youths from cities like Glasgow.

And he had lived a rough life, by any standards. His story started with his entire family dying in a fire. He had survived, aged six, by leaping from a third-storey window on to the concrete pavement below. After recovering from two broken legs, a broken arm and a cracked skull he had been sent to live with an old spinster aunt. Ten years later he ran away, living off what he could steal, which naturally matured an inbred tendency towards pickpocketing. He had been caught twice, red-handed. The first time he had returned to his loathed old aunt. The second, he had done two months' community service, living in a Borstal at night and doing the disgusting jobs no one else would do during the day. He had run away after two months, disappearing into the battered Clydeside slums and deserted shipyards to live with the dregs of Glaswegian humanity and a great many rats.

Sometime during that period he joined a gang of similarly homeless, rootless thugs. He gained control of the ten or so kids, using a mixture of heavy fistwork and an unusual talent for verbally discrediting his opponents. His leadership had been brief, only a couple of weeks, before tragedy struck. The gang had come to blows with its biggest Protestant enemies outside Ibrox after an Old Firm football match. It had been a vicious battle, under the banner of religious loathing. When the police at last succeeded in breaking up the mêlée there were four youths lying half-dead with serious wounds. One had been bottled in the face, scarring him for life; the others had been knifed. The remaining sixteen ran, Callum with a six-inch flick-knife sticking out of his stomach.

Somehow he got himself to a doctor. The wound was patched up in a rudimentary way, but Callum had lost a great deal of blood. When he had finished the doctor asked his patient to wait a minute while he fetched something. Callum guessed correctly that he would be ringing the police and left through the surgery window.

Two days later he turned up, staggering with fatigue and pain, in Oban. There the people guessed that he was no more than a little hooligan, but they harboured him, giving his thin story the benefit of the doubt. The rougher part of Oban, frequented by fishermen and lorry drivers, took the child under its protective wing.

Since then he had become the messenger boy, menial worker and extra bar hand for anyone who needed him. He had come to Oban when he was just sixteen; he was now nearly nineteen. His habits of stealing and fighting had left him, to a degree; not to say, however, that he did not have to be as tough as iron in the company he kept. But, even if he had straightened out he was still dipping into a handsome savings account built on the proceeds of his pilfering. That in itself proved him to be something out of the normal as inner-city teenage ruffians go; whereas most would immediately blow it on glue, or heroin at five quid a shot, Callum saved it. He smoked heavily, as he had for as long as he could remember, but he knew better than to waste even ill-gotten gains.

And, to end his story, told in snatches to Ian during the first three days and liberally spiced up with witticisms, he could never really return to Glasgow, even if he wished to; or at least he could not go back for a long time. One of the boys who had been knifed back at Ibrox had died two days later with severe abdominal wounds. Fourteen of the sixteen who had initially escaped were later caught. As they already had police records as long as their arms it had not been difficult to pick them up. Two of his own gang and three of the other were given nine years for murder and attempted murder. The others got sentences varying from eighteen months to seven years. By a combination of luck and sheer naked ability the two most wanted members of the gangs, both the leaders, had eluded capture totally.

Ian mulled all of this for quite a while and realized that he had caught himself something resembling a shark, rather than the pike he had bargained for. But the fact that Callum told him all of this in good faith put him, to a certain extent, at ease. And there was no doubting that Callum Miller was invaluable. He was about on a par with Emma, a year or two before, when she had first appeared. He was willing and eager to please, which Emma had been, and in a different way still was. But he was almost disconcertingly similar to Jim in method. Although Callum and Jim were utterly different people, with dissimilar backgrounds, there was a resemblance that made Ian come to like him. Their native cunning and instinct for self-preservation, their dry, caustic sense of humour and their barely concealed wildness were the same. And Ian loved Jim as his son and greatest friend, although he would never admit it, even to himself. So Callum, despite his past, had a head start. He was wise enough to realize this and nurture it without pushing too hard.

As the days crawled by Ian found himself worrying about *Blue Dog* more and more. A funny name, *Blue Dog* . . . what was it supposed to mean? Jim and Emma, for some

109

inexplicable reason, had found it amusing. Two or three times, when they had contacted Pirate, there had been a vague, almost imperceptible catch in their voices when they mentioned those two words, as if they were smiling as they said them. It was probably some perverse, slightly warped joke of Jim's. He had always shown an odd sense of humour, designed entirely to half-shock, half-amuse Emma. They would spend hours flinging witticisms at each other, as lovers do. But, with Jim especially, there was always a hint of something close to malice – stronger than impishness but not quite malevolent. It was as if he enjoyed the knowledge that he could run a verbal jig around anyone at any time he wished.

Ian, in his slow, wise way thought about Jim and Emma in an entirely new way. He realized, one night, that they scared hell out of him. This did not detract from his love for them; more, it was accentuated because he guessed shrewdly that they often frightened both themselves and each other too. And now this affair had exploded in all of their faces, like a timebomb which had been destined to go off sooner or later, and Ian did not know what to expect when he next saw them. Strong people can be incredibly brittle when whatever their strength is built on is undermined. Jim's strength came from his mixture of animal cunning and premeditated mischievousness. God knows *that* had been undermined when he killed two people. What kind of fey, dangerous creature would he turn into? That frightened Ian. And Emma's strength came from her ability to lean on Jim and rely on him. But just as a blooming, beautiful tree is as good as dead when the forest that surrounds it dies, if Jim's cool left him, then Emma could not possibly survive.

Ian dearly wanted to contact them, to talk to them and calm his fears. He wanted to know for sure that they were capable of continuing, that they were still sane, that they

110

were not hitting the cocaine too hard – Ian kicked himself over and over again for not confiscating it on Loch Nevis – and, most of all, that their love still thrived and flourished as it had always done.

Contacting them, however, was not at all easy – unless they were within between forty and sixty miles from him, depending on the interference. If they were not within that range all contact had to be done through Radio North-West, which had an aerial capable of reaching a hundred and fifty miles from Oban. But if, for instance, *Blue Dog* was off Northern Lewis and *Rob Roy* was off Islay, nigh on three hundred miles away, contacting was not just a matter of picking up the transmitter and talking. It was a very complicated business. Furthermore the public status of the radio station made it open to anyone who cared to listen in: radio hams, CB enthusiasts and, finally, the police. Luckily, very little of what was said on the air, either by the disc jockeys or by *Rob Roy* and *Blue Dog* when they called in, was of any use at all to eavesdroppers. The calls could be traced, but by the time anyone could get to the places they had come from Jim and Ian were invariably long gone. All the same Jim had always been bad about using the radio and Ian reckoned that his reluctance now bordered on paranoia. He disliked running the risk of having his transmissions eavesdropped on or being traced even when he knew that he was perfectly safe. The longer the chase went on, the more acutely conscious he would become of these hazards and the more inclined he would be to leave the radio alone except in dire emergencies. His periodic contacts with Pirate were sporadic, secretive and deliberately uninformative. And, the longer *Blue Dog* was at sea, the more spasmodic his calls became. The lengths in between each one fairly made Ian's blood run cold. The last call he had heard had come earlier that evening, the third day since he had left Oban.

111

By coincidence it had come over his two-way radio, rather than on the more powerful wireless, which meant that they were close to each other. Ian had weaved out from Oban, towards Islay and Kintyre. Then, after a night in Port Ellen on Islay he swung north again, towards Skye and the Hebrides. He was therefore deeply surprised, about thirty miles south-east of Barra, to hear Emma's voice coming over loud and clear. At first he did not believe that he had actually heard the voice on the two-way radio and waited, leaning towards the radio and listening intently, for a second chance to hear her. It was another fifteen minutes before he caught a jumble of transmissions in which Emma appeared to be participating. He tried to contact *Blue Dog* but for some reason the airwaves were blocked by a great deal of radio contact going on up ahead, fading rapidly into a distance blur. By the time the airwaves cleared *Blue Dog* appeared to have gone out of range. This meant that they were moving away fast and could possibly be up to sixty miles from *Rob Roy* on as clear a day as this. It was mildly frustrating for Ian, but there was nothing to be done. This was the last anyone heard of *Blue Dog* for some time.

On the same night there came ever more frequent warnings of what Pirate was pleased to refer to as 'a float of sea-pigs' in the Minch, heading southwards in a worryingly purposeful way. As Ian had already bypassed Mingulay to the west and there was no time, for a sprint across the Minch to the safety of the mainland sea-lochs, he opted for heading straight on. Navigating without lights, by the eerie, silver sheen shed by a waning moon on the sea and the low islands, he crept up the shore of Mingulay, slipped over to Barra and continued his beach-hugging. He weaved into the islands which lie off the north-eastern corner of Barra and hid in the narrow sound between the islands of Gighay and Hellisay, as good a place as any to hide in the

Outer Hebrides. He was not a moment too soon. Within five minutes of *Rob Roy*'s anchor dropping, four big launches roared by, their bows high in the water, scything through the calm sea. They were following the ferry route between Lochboisdale in South Uist and Castlebay in Barra, passing so close to Ian's hiding place that Callum said he could see the letters emblazoned on the sides of the nearest two boats. Ian nervously asked him to read them out. After some squinting and peering into the half-darkness Callum gave one of them. Ian swore. 'Whit's the matter?' Callum demanded.

Ian was silent for a moment. 'Bugger,' he said quietly. 'I thought they didnae look right.'

'Why? Whit's wrong?' Callum asked in agitation.

'They're no bluidy cops.'

'Whit the fuck are they, then?'

'Militia . . . Thon's a bluidy navy trick, thon.'

'I don't get it,' Callum said, frowning.

'Thon fucking numbers.' Ian was almost shouting in his dismay. 'The polis dinnae hae numbers on their boats, thon's a navy trick.'

'Well?' Callum shouted back.

'*Well?* Well they boats're quicker, better, stronger, bigger an' equipped like the *Ark*-frigging-*Royal*.'

'Oh.'

They may have had policemen in them and meant serious business, or the navy was having some private war game in the Outer Hebrides. The latter was extremely unlikely. The navy and army may think that their war games are top secret, but fishermen always somehow get wind of them at least a week in advance. Callum remarked that it gave him 'the shits'. Ian contemplated this for a while and concluded that it was an apt description. So badly did he 'get the shits' that he came to a rapid decision to take serious evasive action. He steered *Rob Roy* westwards, through the Sound of Fuday and into the great wide Atlantic. Where he was headed no sane-minded person, not even a policeman, would follow.

'Where're we going?' Callum asked.

'Island called St Kilda,' Ian replied from the controls.

'Sounds great . . . where is it?'

'On the edge of the world,' came the helpful answer.

'Oh? What's it like?'

'Remote.'

'Inhabited?' Callum was beginning to adapt to conversations conducted in one-word sentences and monosyllables.

'Few bored militia.'

'Aren't we running frae the militia?'

'Aye.'

'Then why're we going tae St Kelda, or whatever it's called?'

'St Kilda! . . . Cos I ken these ones.'

'They OK?'

Ian sighed and flung a half-despairing, half-angry look at Callum. 'Yer aye esking questions . . . why? why? why? Yer like a wee bairn.'

'I niver get any answers, though,' Callum muttered.

Again Ian sighed. 'We're going tae St Kilda because nae yin else would think o' going there and because I ken the people on it. They run some radar station or something for the army. They're fucking bored because St Kilda's about forty miles frae Uist. They'll put uz up for a night or two until the heat's off of us . . . Enough?'

Callum grinned cockily.

'Aye . . . Ta.'

'Thank God. Now could ye leave us in peace fer a bit?'

'Why?' Callum burst out laughing and had to sit down to regain his composure.

Ian stared at him bleakly. 'Sometimes', he said pensively, 'sometimes, my boy, you get right up my arse.'

'I ken,' Callum replied through a renewed bout of giggles. Ian shook his head, as adults do when faced with children enjoying themselves.

Even with the ocean at its calmest *Rob Roy* made slow progress against the heavy Atlantic surge. They headed up the west coast of South Uist during the night. Unlike many of the coasts which face the full wrath of the Atlantic, South Uist is shadowed by beaches, sand dunes and shallows up its west coast. Ian spent the whole night worrying that a police patrol or worse, the navy launches, would come down the coast. If they did he would have nowhere to hide. The only hope would be to run for the open sea and pray that they did not deem it worthwhile to follow. It was not a position he wished to be in.

But nothing went wrong. At four o'clock Ian stopped at Creagorry, on Benbecula. There he filled up the tanks, bought some supplies and the newspaper and set sail again within the hour. By dawn on Saturday morning the weather was beginning to turn sour. There was a keen, bitter north-easterly blowing up, threatening to batter Scotland with a taste of the arctic winter. Out in the open ocean, as the Hebrides sank into the sea behind there was a defiant effort by the sun to hold off the impending onslaught. For a few hours it shone brightly as the cold, thin wind wound itself up, hurling black clouds out to where a cloudbank lay on the western horizon. And in those brief few hours of sun Ian saw eight aeroplanes and two helicopters. He became nervous. There was nowhere with an airport between *Rob Roy* and Nova Scotia; and these were not jetliners. Luckily the helicopters were staying nearer to the archipelago, afraid of the impending storm. But Ian recognized two jet aircraft as RAF reconnaissance planes. They had evil-looking apparatus on them, especially on the tail. One flew directly overhead, about a thousand feet up.

'Nimrod,' Callum remarked.

'You what?'

'Nimrod,' Callum explained. 'Can take a photo of a pimple on yer arse frae ten thousand feet.'

'Get below,' Ian ordered.

'What?'

'*Get below*. I'm supposed tae be alone.'

'Ye dinnae think they're aifter us, I mean . . .'

'Get below,' Ian ordered a third time. 'I'm no taking the risk.'

By midday the sky was black, hanging over the increasingly turbulent sea like a bad dream. The aeroplanes appeared to have given up. Callum had not before seen Ian using only the compass to navigate. It made him distinctly uneasy. He spent long hours glancing nervously at the huge waves and at the sky and listening to the creaking of the boat as it seemed to disappear into a whole new universe. He spent much of the rest of the time staring ahead, hoping to see some indication of land. He repeatedly asked Ian if they were close. Ian's answers were enigmatic, as if he were not entirely sure. At about one o'clock Callum asked the same question, quietly, shyly – like a child who is embarrassed to admit that he mistrusted the judgement of an adult.

'Are we close yet, Mister MacGillavray? The sea's getting awful rough, though.'

'Aye, we're close. And if ye think it's rough now ye'll be glad no tae be in it in an hour or two. Its just warming up yet.'

They reached the haven of St Kilda, a small permanently embattled bastion of seven islands, isolated forty miles West of Toe Head on Harris. Callum almost cried for joy when they rounded Levenish and headed into the sheltered harbour and dropped the anchor in the heaving seas. The wind was howling like thousands of maddened wolves. St Kilda was shrouded in cloud – dead, empty, solitary.

Callum and Ian gathered some provisions together and rowed ashore. They beached the dinghy and followed a thin path up to a village of low, peat-roofed houses. They were built like drystone dykes, with stones of any shape and size cunningly fitted together like oversized, intricate puzzles. Most of the houses were derelict, varying from heaps of rubble to reclaimable but uncomfortable-looking shacks. A few, three or four in the centre of the village, were strong and intact. Smoke billowed from their low chimneys and their lights glowed. Amongst the general decay they were heartwarming sights.

Ian walked to the nearest and largest. It was a bungalow, like the rest, but larger and wider. Perhaps it had been the head man's home when there still was a population on St Kilda, before late-Victorian tourists innocently destroyed the solitude of the islanders. It must have been a rough life, living off the meat of sea birds and the annual supply of grain from the Hebrides. But, although it was no idyll and certainly not the pretentious, Kitsch idea of paradise that the Victorians bequeathed to later generations of foolish mainlanders, it was free and untainted, or at least it had been before tourism turned its livelihood into a souvenir economy. *Then* it became Kitsch . . . and died. And now only the houses remained as monuments to primitive crofters who had lived and survived, despite the outside world, beyond their time.

Ian knocked on the door and entered. Callum followed, taking in the room at a glance. There was only one room, thirty feet long and twenty feet wide. At one end a coal fire roared. There was a long table down the centre of the room, covered in discarded books and newspapers, plates

117

of half-eaten food, cigarette packets. A huge, quadruple-size bottle of whisky sat proudly in the centre. It took no genius to guess what one object the bored men relied on most. The bottle was almost empty. By the fire were two huge sofas and four large, comfortable armchairs. For such a big room it was surprisingly cosy. Ian and Callum were immediately drawn to the fire. When they reached it they noticed, for the first time, an inert, slumbering body sprawled on one of the sofas. Ian cleared his throat. No reaction.

'Captain MacKay?'

Still no reaction.

'Captain MacKay?'

One eye of the prostrate man opened languidly and inspected the intruder. The eye closed. A few seconds later both eyes opened. The man slowly pulled himself to a sitting position, put his head in his hands and groaned.

'Fuck,' he wheezed. Callum moved over to the fire and stretched out his hands, drinking in the warmth. MacKay stood up shakily and inspected Ian again. He ran a hand across one unshaven cheek and into his unkempt brown hair.

'Ian?' he asked, as if he could not see the man who stood in front of him.

'Aye.'

Exhausted by his efforts MacKay slumped back on to the sofa. 'Christ, I feel awful.'

'Ye dinnae look sae guid.'

'Thanks.'

'Had a piss-up?' The captain looked up and studied Ian for a second before letting his head drop again. He raised it, let it drop again, raised it again and let it drop. It was not one of the most vigorous nods ever witnessed, but it appeared to take a lot out of him.

'Fuck-all else to do,' he murmured.

*

They had a piss-up that night. Captain MacKay revived after a few drinks, and his four companions were happy to join in. Ian had brought three bottles, knowing that whisky, if nothing else, would buy their favour. They had been on St Kilda for a month and had another two weeks to go. Two weeks is a lifetime on a place like St Kilda, where more people go stark-staring mad, become irredeemable drunks and learn to hate people, as well as the place itself, in those last two weeks than in every other fortnight of their lives. St Kilda was treated by the Ministry of Defence as a sort of endurance test. An Outward Bound course for the most resilient of its employees. In three years two people had so got into the swing of things that they had bounded outwards in style. One had bounded off the edge of a cliff on Boreray, one of the seven islands. The other had tried to row home and was never seen again. The MOD, with typical bureaucratic brilliance, liked the six-week stint too much to change it just because of a couple of suicides and a few lushes. It was all a matter of staying power, they said. It sure was, MacKay said.

As the storm outside screamed and wailed, buffeting the small house as if it were the victim of some cosmic pillow fight, the seven people drank all three bottles. Ian recounted the story of the cocaine and everything that had happened after the finding of it. They had heard the news on the radio. To Ian's surprise it amused rather than shocked them. They wanted to see the newspaper Ian had bought on Benbecula. Neither Ian nor Callum had bothered to read it. When they looked at it now they got a shock.

It was a Fleet-Street tabloid. The headline on the third page ran: 'Battle of Camusrory. New Findings'.

A smaller headline read: 'Latest on the Drug War Shoot-out in the West of Scotland'.

It said, in fact, very little more than *The Western Gazette* had said on Tuesday. Two trawlers and three people were being chased around the Western Isles, 'wanted for questioning in connection with the Camusrory incident', to use the exact words of the police. It seemed absurd that they should stick to that hackneyed phraseology. Who would mount a full-scale operation, in conjunction with the navy and RAF, to question someone in connection with something?

'Why not just say that they're chasing you because they want to nobble you?' one of the men offered. Ian was too flabbergasted by the article to reply.

One thing that the police had found out, or perhaps had at last admitted, was that Jim MacGregor was the other man. They still had not succeeded in working out who, or what, Emma was.

At some point during the night one of the men was woken up by the telephone.

'Hello?' he groaned.

'St Kilda?'

'Well, it's not fucking Johannesburg,' he grumbled.

'This is Base.'

'This is quarter to five.'

'Sorry to disturb you.'

'So you should be.'

After that Base went into a monologue which lasted five minutes. When he had finished he was treated to a few more insults, then both ends hung up.

'Who was that?' Ian muttered. He had been sleeping next to the telephone.

'Base!'

'What they want?'

'Boat called *Rob Roy*. Said it was headed this way. I told them it had prob'ly sunk. They're sending out a helicopter tomorrow, weather permitting, and a few launches.'

Ian turned over, closing his eyes again. 'Shit,' he murmured before falling asleep again.

When they awoke the next morning the weather was grey and bleak and the wind was strong, but the worst of the gale had passed over. It was Sunday morning. Two hundred miles away, at Thurso, *Blue Dog* was heading out towards Orkney even as *Rob Roy* quit St Kilda and set course for Mingulay.

With the huge Atlantic surge thrusting them back towards Scotland as if the boat were a motorized surfboard, *Rob Roy* made good headway. At about ten o'clock they saw the tiny rocks of Haskeir Eagach and swung south towards the Monach Islands, ten miles west of North Uist. Four launches rounded the headland of Grimmish Point and gave chase. They had been waiting.

It was a well-sprung trap. They were the same boats that had made Ian so nervous two nights before, fast and sleek. They fanned out, forcing *Rob Roy* to run south down the coasts of Benbecula and South Uist. Ian swerved out to sea, not wishing to be hemmed in against the beaches. The launches moved with him, creeping closer and closer. He cut back in and began to make wide, shallow tacks backwards and forwards, now out to sea, now right in, close to the land.

Ian had one advantage. He could not shake off his pursuers in broad daylight, but his reputation said that he could. As Uist drew to its southern end two of the launches banked away to the left, covering any attempts he might make to slip through the Sound of Barra. He slewed heavily out to sea, apparently deterred. The launches moved to rescue their former positions, one off the port bows, just out of range for accurate rifle shooting, the other at the same distance off the port stern. As they manoeuvred themselves into position Ian made his bid. He swerved back towards Barra, neatly cutting in between both boats, and

121

swung around Fiaray into the Sound of Fuday. The boat behind immediately gave chase, the other three were forced to retrace the previous mile or so. There was time to spare, not much time, but enough to push the advantage. And Ian was in his element now: sandbanks, reefs and small islands. He cut northwards around Fuday, pulling his enemy with him, crossed the Sound of Barra and entered the Sound of Eriskay. But short of Eriskay he again turned back on himself, re-crossing the Sound of Barra. The radio crackled with conflicting orders, directions and distances. Ian made a final swerve, running into the sound between Gighay and Hellisay, where he had hidden from the same launches two nights before. Two boats followed him but were forced to turn back when they realized that they could not navigate the shallows. Ian himself slipped out of the sound and raced out into the Sea of the Hebrides, heading for Rhum. He had ten minutes' grace before the launches organized themselves.

It took three hours to cross the sound to the Inner Hebrides. By then it was two o'clock in the afternoon. The launches had gained no ground, staying back in case Ian decided to play more games. He made a beeline for the Sound of Canna, between Rhum and Canna, and turned north towards the safety of Skye, slowing up as he did. The pursuers drew up until they were close enough to see Ian's face. Then he cut between the two who shadowed him to the south, accelerating down the east coast of Rhum. They gave chase once more.

He feinted towards the Sound of Rhum when the cliffs of that island fell away at the southern end, made a second feint towards Skye and sped around the coast of Eigg. Ian was beginning to enjoy himself. He knew now that he could beat these boats if he tried. He swung into the harbour of Galmisdale on Eigg and waited. Two of the launches motored by, then a third curved into the harbour. It slowed up, beginning to turn back out to sea before its crew spotted *Rob Roy*. Ian had hugged the cliffs of the island which stands in the harbour mouth. When the navy launch slowed up he pulled his throttle full out and raced towards it. The navy saw the intent of the trawler seconds before she smashed into their side. There was nothing they could do but watch in horror as *Rob Roy* plunged into them, breaking the metal side like plywood. Ian turned and headed for Muck, leaving the bemused, angry sailors to swim for the shore.

'Three tae one,' Callum remarked, speaking for the first time in hours, ' . . . nae bother.'

Ian grinned. 'Fun, eh?'

'Aye. I like the fitba more, though.'

'No fer me. Too tame,' Ian remarked before sinking back into his habitual silence of concentration.

He needed petrol so he stopped in Port Mor, on Muck. The radio informed them that the navy launches were turning back, having overshot Rhum by some distance. Ian waited for them to close in before accelerating towards the lighthouse which was now winking north of Coll. Two of the launches gave chase, one having stopped in Port Mor for fuel. To their eternal credit the people who sold diesel on Muck succeeded in mixing about five pounds of sugar in with the petrol. Ten minutes after leaving the harbour the odds were down to two to one; the third launch was rocking up and down, totally incapacitated somewhere between Muck and Ardnamurchan.

The light was now beginning to fade and the navy made a final, despairing bid to catch their elusive prey. The chase sped down Western Coll and out in between Coll and Tiree. Ian had one last trick left up his sleeve before night came. All day he had been on ground he did not know particularly well. But now, only five hours from Oban, he was in his own back yard. He knew this area so well that

123

he could have done it blindfold. He waited until the pincer was on top of him, then made a neat, right-angled turn for Mull. Three hundred yards behind the launches did the same, making to cut him off about a mile out to sea, where he had no chance of escape. For a few minutes Ian steered on, ordering Callum to keep a sharp eye on the pursuers.

There is a famously treacherous reef off Tiree which submerges just below the surface at high tide. No one in their right mind crosses it without knowing precisely where it breaks into deep ruts. Ian knew exactly what he was doing and executed the crossing perfectly. The launches, however, were so eager to catch their prey that they did not bother to look and see where they were. The first they knew of the reef was when the foremost launch struck it travelling at about thirty knots. Callum, who was watching through the binoculars, shrieked as the boat lurched to a halt, its nose diving under the waves. It pivoted like a toy for a few minutes, tearing a great gash through the hull. The second boat reluctantly pulled up to pick up their furious friends as they dived clear. Bound by necessity over duty, it gave up the chase. After two or three minutes the wrecked boat, hit by the wash of its friend, lurched forward, hovered for a moment and slid under the waves.

'*Wow!*' Callum yelled, 'we're the wee boys. *Wow, wooooeeee!*' He capered around the cabin shouting for joy.

All day the pursuers had been cocksure; when Ian ruined the first boat they had been angry. When the second one ground to a halt they had been even more furious. But now that all evaporated. One brief exchange, between the one survivor and their base in Oban, summed up their utter dejection.

'Alpha Two-oh. Base, do you read? Over.'

'We read you, Alpha two-oh.'

'He got away.'

'*You what?*'

124

'He did it again. A reef by Tiree. Beta's sunk.'

'Oh shit.'

Callum spun to Ian, who was studying his handiwork with undisguised pleasure.

'Ye clever auld bastard.'

Ian nodded modestly.

'How d'ye ken they'd hit it?'

'I didnae.'

Callum shook his head, still staring at Ian. He blew out a long, thin stream of smoke from pursed lips. 'Man, thon wis worth a day o' puking ony time. I'll tell *thon* tae ma bairns some day.'

'Mebbe,' said Ian. 'Mebbe no. We're no out o' this yet.'

They reached Mull at dusk and anchored at Dervaig, a small hamlet about ten miles by road from Tobermory. They slept soundly in the knowledge that, after a day-long chase from somewhere near Benbecula, down to Barra, across to Rhum, Eigg and then Muck, then to Tiree and Coll, they had successfully made complete fools of the navy.

Callum rose shortly after dawn and obtained Ian's permission to go into Tobermory to buy cigarettes. He rowed to the shore and hitched a lift into town. Ian turned over and fell asleep again.

He rose again at ten, ate a hearty breakfast and tried to obtain some news of *Blue Dog* through Pirate. Nothing. After that he began to write up his private log, which had fallen into disuse in the past few days. He wrote, made himself a cup of coffee, wrote, relaxed, smoked another cigarette and wrote a bit more. He had just looked at his watch and, having found that it was already quarter to twelve, was scolding himself for being lazy when Callum's voice wafted across the water. Ian stood up and looked towards the shore. Callum was rowing like someone possessed, curving the oars deep into the water in strokes that were so heavy that each one lifted him out of his

125

seat. He was shouting something unintelligible. Ian rapidly checked the instruments and dials around the controls to make sure everything was ready for a hasty retreat. He quietly cursed the boy for finding trouble and, most probably, bringing it with him. Then he ran out on to the deck and leaned over, waiting for Callum to reach him. In a few more strokes he was level with the cabin. He dropped the oars, gasping for breath, sweat running in rivers down his back.

'Whit's the matter?' Ian demanded.

Callum reached to the floor of the dinghy and hurled a newspaper on to the deck. 'Read that,' he panted.

Ian opened it out. It was the biggest-selling daily paper in Scotland, the *Daily Tribune*. On the front page was a hazy picture of Jim, aged seventeen, a photo of a letter in Jim's handwriting and a typewritten crib beside it. The banner headline read:

DRUG KILLINGS – JAMES MACGREGOR SPEAKS OUT.
A *Daily Tribune* Exclusive

Ian sat down and read the article until he came to Jim's beautifully written epistle. Although it was much smaller than the typescript beside it, only displayed so as to prove it's authenticity, Ian read it in preference to the type translation. It said this:

To the Editor of the Daily Tribune
Dear Sir,
I write to you in desperation, as the last and only hope I can think of for stating my case and trying to explain what really happened at Camusrory.

Last Saturday night, while fishing in Loch Hourn off Knoydart, myself and two friends picked up what we took to be a lobster pot, which turned out to be full of a large quantity of cocaine. That night and through the next day we were chased

126

constantly and fired at repeatedly. In the course of defending myself and my friends I, James MacGregor, fired back.

I am writing now to say that I would gladly come in at the first opportunity to answer any charges levelled against me. However, I will not do this until I know that some attempt is being made to arrest the people who were shooting at me. It seems as if the police are more interested in catching a scapegoat than in catching the plague of drug smugglers and criminals who still roam free on the west coast. I would ask them to contemplate the remote possibility that it might take two sides to make a gunfight.

Thus, as I believe that whatever I did was done in self-defence, and would freely admit to it in an 'impartial' court of law, I can see no sane or fair reason why Ian MacGillavray and my cousin Robert should have to shoulder the burden of my guilt.

I realize that I am in no position to threaten anyone, but I have this warning for everyone who might intend to harass us any more: only an amnesty for Ian and Rob could end this ridiculous boat chase. And if it goes on more people could die needlessly. Before you make a decision I would ask you to consider who will take the blame for them.

Yours
 James MacGregor
 Lord Assynt

The *Daily Tribune* had devoted not only a great deal of the front page, but also the centre spread, to this story.

Jim had chosen well. The *Scotsman* would have disapproved, at best giving the article a little space, tucked away amongst the cats-saved-by-local-fire-brigade-in-Corstorphine-type articles. Fleet Street would have ignored or edited it, to fit their own specifications. But the *Daily Tribune* loved this kind of story. A true-blue Scottish tale of injustice and woe. It did not edit one word, giving the

127

story full coverage as well as accompanying it with a brief article analysing the points Jim had made. The editor had obviously made a snap decision, not knowing whether Jim had sent the letter to other newspapers. The *Tribune* printed the story as soon as they could, giving Jim the benefit of the doubt and believing that he was what he said he was: innocent. Half an hour after the paper hit the stands, half of Scotland – at a liberal estimate – would know about Jim's letter. By the end of Monday morning the sympathy aroused for *Rob Roy* and *Blue Dog* would be overwhelming.

And that is exactly what happened. Public indignation and anger grew rapidly. Here were injustice, drugs, murder and enough enigma to keep speculation going. Jim had chosen well in opting for the *Tribune*, and the *Tribune* in turn had dealt with the scoop perfectly. Both could only gain from the printing of the letter.

Ian finished the article and stood up. He had pored over it, slowly and carefully, trying to find some motive behind it. He gave the paper to Callum and sighed.

'He's got guts, yer lord. I'll gi' 'im that,' Callum remarked.

Ian nodded, biting a thumbnail pensively. 'Aye. He's got guts.'

'Whit gets me,' Callum continued musingly, ' . . . is how yon clever bugger got 'imself tae Thurso by Friday morn.'

'What d'you mean?'

'Hiv ye no read the piece on it? Thon envelope wis stamped frae Thurso.'

'Beats me,' said Ian distractedly. He walked slowly back to the cabin.

'Aye, he's got guts,' he muttered to himself.

Emma stormed into the bedroom of the hotel where they were staying, as husband and wife, in Stromness on Orkney. She stomped to the basin where Jim was shaving and slammed a newspaper down beside him. He jumped, cut himself and swore.

'What was that for? You made me cut myself.'

Emma glared at him, clenching her fists in anger. 'What kind of disloyal, fickle, fair-weather schoolgirl d'you think I am?' she demanded hotly.

Jim looked up, arching his black eyebrows in surprise. 'Fickle? . . . Fair-weather . . . Don't tell me, let me guess . . .'

'Don't be frivolous with me, James MacGregor. I want a straight answer . . . *Now!*'

'First, would you be so kind as to inform me what the fuck you're on about?'

'This.' She jabbed at the newspaper. Jim glanced at it and nodded. He went back to his shaving.

'Well?' she asked acidly.

'I find it very surprising they got it so quickly. Perhaps it's something to do with the oilmen only being allowed off the rigs at the weekend.' He smiled sweetly and finished off his shaving.

'Why. Did. You. Write. *That. Letter?*' Emma spelt out, her voice rising.

'Think about it,' Jim answered calmly.

'I have.'

'Good, then you'll have worked out that I just ensured an amnesty for you and Ian if it works . . . If I know the *Tribune.*'

'Did it occur to you that I might not want an amnesty?' Emma asked. 'Did it occur to you that I wouldn't be here with you unless I lov . . .' She stopped, blushed slightly and corrected herself, ' . . . I wanted to be here.'

Jim sighed and carefully placed the razor on the side of the basin. 'Yes,' he said. 'Yes, in fact it did. But then did it occur to you that Ian probably does?' She stared at him, unanswering, so he continued. 'I actually weighed up all the possibilities, though you may not believe it. As it stands at the moment you and Ian are both carrying a third of the responsibility for something I did. If, and I stress if, this works, then what you do from then on is your decision and your problem. At least if you've been offered an amnesty you can say that I coerced you into staying, or maybe plead insanity, or love, or whatever. It's my guilt and I'm not going to have you condemned for it.'

'If you go to prison, I'm going too,' she replied.

Jim wiped his face with a hand towel, took a cigarette from a packet lying on a low table and lit it. He looked at Emma for a moment before speaking. 'You know, that's possibly the stupidest thing I've ever heard.'

Emma sat down heavily on the bed, deflated and pouting.

Jim continued, 'You go to a women's prison, me to a men's prison. We both do . . . what? . . . ten years perhaps; maybe five or six with good behaviour. You for something you didn't even do. And we wouldn't even be able to see each other. Fantastic. At least if you're free you could visit me every now and again.'

'Do you want me to stay with you, though?' Emma asked quietly, still pouting.

Jim laughed quickly and, pulling her to her feet, enveloped her in a tight hug. 'Do wild bears shit in the woods?'

There was a long silence. At last Emma sighed. 'You're right, as usual.'

'My love, don't get pissed off. You wouldn't fit in gaol, you're far too pretty. What kind of a lover would I be if I allowed you to go through being shorn, given a number and locked up with a lot of psychopathic lesbians?'

He said all of this with a half-smile. His voice was both soothing and vaguely amused. Emma could not help smiling at his description of women's prisons.

'You're not going to give yourself up, though?' she asked.

130

Jim laughed. 'God, *no*. I'm going to be a bloody legend.'

Emma in turn laughed. 'Arrogant bastard.'

The smile that Jim flung at her was almost demonic. He stretched his arms, flexing his shoulder muscles. Turning to the window he spoke quietly. 'Mebbe . . . Mebbe no.'

Amnesty

When the Secretary of State for Scotland flew north to Edinburgh on the Monday morning the reports of what was happening on the west coast had seemed a million miles away, the exaggerated and hysterical over-reactions of a backwoods police force who wouldn't have recognized crime if it came up and stabbed them in the back. Far greater on his list of priorities was the meeting he was scheduled to have with a delegation of miners over the planned closure of a pit in Fife.

But no sooner had he reached his office than he began to understand fully what a godawful mess this Camusrory affair actually was. The papers could talk of nothing else, giving MacGregor, a good-looking boy by all accounts, the sort of coverage usually reserved for pop singers and royalty. They lionized him, accusing everyone but the boy himself of all manner of crimes, including dirty tricks, harassment and even corruption.

Added to this, the whole of that morning and the afternoon which the Secretary of State had specifically put aside for preparing a speech to the miners, were spent trying to pour oil on a sea of indignant invective coming in from all over Scotland. MPs, even one or two from his own party, were quick to make a moral issue of the affair; they all said a great deal without being at all helpful. And, after a few hours of consideration the Secretary of State was forced to admit that they had a point. There was something peculiar going on and there did seem to be more to this than immediately met the eye. He could not quite put his finger on what was wrong, but he knew with the instinct of a true politician that if the police were not exactly barking up the wrong tree then they were certainly nowhere near the right one. Even though the Secretary of State was becoming used to this kind of thing happening every time he came north, this one seemed slightly out of the norm. He was sceptical of the rumours of police complicity in the drug smuggling, but there was a vague, nagging suspicion that they were more than reluctant to find out what had really happened at Camusrory. This in turn seemed to suggest, as one newspaper commented, that Jim MacGregor had accidentally contravened a tacit *laissez-faire* between the police and the smugglers and was suffering for his folly.

Another peculiarity caught his attention later on in the day. He had given up even hoping that he would be able to prepare some coherent notes for his ordeal with the miners and was poring over a newspaper. There was an article about the recent spate of drug smuggling on the west coast and, not surprisingly, there was a picture of MacGregor to complement the piece. It was this, rather than the somewhat dull article, that caught his attention. There were two people in the picture, both in their early twenties. The Secretary of State read the caption and was surprised to see the names of James and Robert MacGregor. He was even more amazed when it dawned on him that this was *the* Robert MacGregor; the almost unfailingly camera-shy one who was assumed by the police to be the shadowy and probably unpleasant criminal acting with James MacGregor. The more he looked at the picture the surer he became. The photograph was all wrong; 'Robert MacGregor' was standing in a way unlike any man would stand, holding a cigarette in a manner which was

133

both effete and peculiarly natural, not the affectation of a homosexual. If this person *was* in fact James MacGregor's lover, as some had speculated, then it appeared that he was the closest thing to a woman MacGregor could have found.

The Secretary of State was sufficiently intrigued to pick up the telephone and ring the chief of the Strathclyde Police to communicate his unease.

On Tuesday morning the Sectreary of State was awoken from a brief but heavy slumber by the telephone. He reached out and brought the receiver into his warm, subterranean cave under the blankets.

'Yes?' he said muzzily. 'What time is it?'

'Seven o'clock, Minister, I'm sorry if I woke you up. It's Jack MacCrinnon.' The minister made slightly halfhearted 'no, don't worry' noises to the chief of the Strathclyde Police.

'We've been so damned stupid,' the latter went on. 'It's been glaring my men in the face for a week.'

The minister yawned cavernously. 'What has, old boy?' he said tonelessly.

'Robert MacGregor, in the Camusrory case?' He said it with a hint of question in his voice, as if he were unsure whether the minister either remembered or cared about Robert MacGregor. He need not have worried. The Secretary of State sat up sharply, suddenly awake, sending a cascade of blankets to the floor.

'Yes, go on.'

'Well we've been looking in the wrong place, sir. We've had an APB out for a young man, eighteen to twenty-four, slight build, blond, possibly homosexual. We didn't even contemplate the alternative until you suggested it last night.

134

'I did?' said the minister, slightly confused. 'What was this alternative?'

'He's not a man, he's a woman dressed to look like a man.'

The minister thought for a moment and a slow frown crawled onto his face. 'But why would a woman want to do that?'

'I'll tell you in a minute, sir. It's just that having hazarded the guess that she was a girl it cut the print possibilities down by half. One of my men just rang me, we've got them.'

For a second the minister wondered whether he was being spectacularly obtuse and then he forged on regardless. 'Got what?'

'Her prints. She was up on a minor drug charge in London a few years back; in the papers and everything. Deb of the year done for possessing cocaine.' He said this last bit in such a meaningful way that the minister was forced to admit that it sounded good so far. Besides, he had a vague recollection of one of his colleagues trying to extricate a wayward son from a similar-sounding case.

'She's called Emma Gaynor,' the chief of police went on, 'Twenty-two, blonde, good-looking; fits the description exactly and . . .' The minister sensed the momentary pause before the *coup de grâce* which was to come:

' . . . We called her parents and apparently she's been living with MacGregor in Argyll for the last three years.'

'Bingo', said the minister. 'So why pretend to be a man?'

'Well sir, this may sound a little odd,' the chief said, sounding slightly embarrassed.

'Yes?'

'Well, we rang up the inspector in Oban and he was adamant that it's inconceivable that it's a girl.'

'Why?'

'He said that no trawlerman would take a woman on

135

board; it's considered bad form, even bad luck, sort of superstition.'

'And if they did?'

'They'd keep it very quiet,' he replied immediately. 'I think, maybe, we have the answer to *one* of our problems, at least.'

Despite himself the Secretary of State grinned. 'Yes, I think we probably do.' He thought for a moment, frowning. 'Listen, Jack, do me a favour and withhold this for a bit.'

'Sorry sir?' He sounded confused.

Still slightly fuddled by sleep the minister came out with something which had been worrying him all through the previous day. He had a sense of foreboding, some politician's sixth sense warning him that such a tangled web as this had to claim more victims before it somehow resolved itself.

'Withhold it. Maybe MacGregor was telling the truth in that letter, in which case they're in a great deal of danger.'

'But they're wanted for murder, sir.'

'Not the girl, if MacGregor's to be believed. She and the old man, MacGillavray, might've just been caught up in something they can't get out of. I think it wouldn't do any harm to preserve her anonymity a little longer.'

'All right, sir, I'll tell my men but we'll keep it from the press.' He thought for a second and laughed quickly. 'Besides, I've never seen any harm in keeping the media out of police business.'

The minister smiled. 'Good man,' he said. 'Trust me. Remember the boy's letter; it takes two sides to make a gunfight.'

A quarter of an hour later the minister was back on the telephone to the chief of the Strathclyde Police. He had given the bizarre goings-on up north a few minutes' thought and it had occurred to him that these three happy-go-lucky poachers were in very serious trouble indeed,

136

probably more serious than even they realized. They were far out of their league and it was imperative that they were extricated and got out of harm's way before the smugglers caught up with them. This was even more necessary if MacGregor was to be believed and his two friends were innocent.

After a short conversation they agreed on the need for an immediate amnesty for Ian MacGillavray and Emma Gaynor, before it was too late.

It was Tuesday morning in Shetland, where Jim and Emma had run: after the letter, postmarked from Thurso, Orkney was not a safe place. Jim was nervous about staying as close, even, as Gutcher on Yell, the second-most northerly of the Shetland Islands. But they both needed rest and inactivity before they began a new run.

They had spent the time calmly and objectively discussing their predicament. They quickly discarded the idea that they could, quite easily, make for the continent from Shetland. But neither of them wanted to do that. Their chances lay in keeping public opinion in Scotland on the boil. If they ran to Norway or Denmark that hope would die. They discussed taking to dry land, a thought that was harder to put aside. Although the sea was a dangerous place for *Blue Dog*, it was their chosen location for this game of hide and seek and they were winning the game so far. To compromise their advantage of being able to play by their own rules would be to put themselves in precisely the same position as the police were in at sea. They also debated the possibility of going to ground until the trouble blew over. But this, they knew, was naive and unrealistic. Sooner or later they would have to emerge, if they were not to live the rest of their lives like hunted animals. Then they would be arrested, tried and sentenced, just as they would have been had they stayed at sea. The

137

main difference would have been that heroes do not run away or hide . . . No, they continue to fight like utter fools, right up to the end. The whole point of Jim's letter to the *Tribune* was to cultivate the image of being the good guys, heroic and tough, fighting a mass of baddies. That, too, was an advantage they could not afford to give up.

So they argued themselves in a full circle until they were back where they had started. They would continue as they had begun and wait as long as it took for Fate to come up with more satisfactory conclusions.

Fate, as is her wont, was unpredictable. The first vital thing came on the Tuesday morning. Jim's letter had set a ball rolling which gathered momentum with remarkable speed. They were happily watching television in bed when the news came on. The first, main story was a live press conference. A man was sitting alone behind a large desk with a map of Western Scotland behind him. He was the civil-servant type: small, bespectacled, balding and dressed in a very expensive, somewhat drab suit. He leant forward, speaking into three microphones. He read out the terms of the amnesty and gave a quick résumé of the reasons for this decision.

Ian was forgiven, free to come in whenever he liked. Emma, who was referred to as 'Lord Assynt's friend, Emma MacGregor', was given full amnesty too, 'if and when she comes in with MacGregor'. The sooner they gave themselves up the more generous the authorities were likely to be.

When it had finished Jim climbed out of bed and turned off the television. He returned to the end of the bed, his face emotionless. For a moment he stood, silent and pensive. Then he lifted the tray of empty cups, jam-smeared plates and crumbs off the table which rested against the end of the bed. Carefully he placed it on another table by the door. When he turned back to the bed a smile was beginning to creep on to his face. His eyes sparkled jubilantly.

'So simple,' he remarked, shaking his head. 'So bloody simple.'

'Doesn't get you off the hook, though . . . or me, for that matter,' Emma replied calmly.

'But Ian's free, though. And I'll bet they know who you are and they're giving you a bloody great bolt-hole, just like I hoped they would . . . It worked.'

'D'you think they know my name?' Emma said ruminatively.

'They know half of it. Or they know all of it and they're keeping the other half quiet.'

At last Emma deigned to smile. She looked at Jim, her eyes sparkling. 'You've got them, haven't you?'

'*We've* got them.'

One of the first lessons to be learnt in life is that Fate does not give without taking away. In his jubilation Jim completely forgot his admirably realistic and long-standing motto, which was that very few silver linings indeed come without big, black clouds. Three hundred and fifty miles away to the south-west in Oban, one of those terrible, appalling twists of fate which make life so unpredictable was forming.

Ian thought hard about that letter in the paper. He was not a stupid man. In his own narrow, xenophobic area he was the wisest man on the west coast. But his mind worked slowly, especially on such things where Jim reacted instinctively. When it came to trying to contemplate what had prompted Jim to write that letter, Ian had to grapple with a very intricate problem – the way Jim's mind worked. Had he foreseen either *Rob Roy* or *Blue Dog* being caught in the near future? Had he panicked, deciding to shoulder the entire blame himself? Ian was thinking this out loud, over a cup of coffee somewhere between Coll and Muck, when Callum asked a very pertinent question.

'Why d'ye run anywise, Mister MacGillavray? Ye've got nought tae hide.'

'Because I was being chased,' he replied immediately. This was true, as far as it went. In the heat of the moment there had been no time for thought, they had done what seemed necessary and had been doing the same ever since.

'But if yer lord's cleared yer name surely yer free tae go hame now?' Callum asked.

Ian did not answer. He did not know the answer. All of that Monday night, long after Callum had fallen asleep, Ian had wrestled with the problem. Now Callum's question precipitated the answer. Ian's mind was clear, he knew what he must do.

He turned *Rob Roy* around and swung into the Sound of Canna. He had nothing to hide, he had an alibi. He radioed Pirate for the last time and told them he was headed for Mallaig. He was going home.

The simple four words – 'I'm going for Mallaig' – echoed around the west coast. The fishermen heard, the populace of Mallaig heard, the police heard.

By some oversight or incompetence the news of the projected amnesty had left the office of the Strathclyde Police at eight o'clock on Tuesday morning but had never got any further. Certainly no one in Oban knew anything about any amnesty. And as for Mallaig, even if Oban had known it would have been a small miracle if anyone got through on the telephone, let alone succeeded in making any impression on the hysteria generated by the news that Ian MacGillavray was 'coming in'.

To add to the confusion the incumbent inspector of the

Mallaig Police who, until recently, had considered a drunken brawl to be the lunatic fringe of crime in his area, desperately tried to convince the hard-headed and heavily armed cops imported from Glasgow that MacGillavray was not dangerous. They listened but refused to be convinced.

'Why take the risk?' they said.

The people of Mallaig acted as one, as anyone on the west coast would have acted, had they been in the same position, when they heard the news about Ian. He was coming in, to them, his family. Nobody on earth could stop them from gathering into a crowd worthy of taking Ian MacGillavray into its collective arms and protecting him from all comers. They admired him, they were proud of him and he was their own.

It was ten o'clock and a large crowd had gathered on the jetty. They were cheering, chanting '*Rob Roy. Rob Roy.*' The police were nervous. They had four boats flanking the mouth of the harbour making a narrow passage through which *Rob Roy* had to pass. They had heard the signal and were unsure what it meant.

At ten minutes to ten *Rob Roy* chugged into sight and the cheering redoubled.

'*Give us* an R,' someone yelled.

'R'.

The trawler drew level with the police launches and it could be seen that there were two people on board.

'*Give us* an O.'

'O' the crowd bawled.

It slowed up. Ian MacGillavray gave the controls to his companion. The nearest police boat, lined with men nervously pointing rifles at the small trawler, was only twenty yards to the right.

'*Give us* a B.'

'B'.

141

Ian appeared from the cabin, holding a rifle. He raised it in salute to the jetty.

'*Give us* an R.'

'R'.

Ian fired a round into the air. Whether a sweat-greasy finger slipped, or nerves made someone react instinctively, or whatever, a man on the furthest-away police boat, who could see only Ian's torso through the cabin window, fired a shot. In the barrage that followed Ian was hit five times, hurling him across the deck. There was dead silence. The crowd were stunned, the policemen on the nearest launch looked horrified. There was a clatter as a rifle fell from a hand, limp with shock.

In a sort of terrible slow motion the crowd and the innocent policemen saw the tragedy. Ian was hurled across the deck by the force of the impact, landing with a crash against the side of the boat. Callum, hit in the shoulder and stomach, jack-knifed through the bridgescreen in an explosion of glass. Out of control *Rob Roy* swerved and ran, head-on, into the left-hand upright pillar which stood at the mouth of the harbour. The bows caved in and water gushed through, tilting the boat down. The nearest police boat rushed in and picked up the two people before *Rob Roy* hovered, tilted, her stern lifting above the slight surge. Then, with the utmost dignity, she sank.

There was nothing to be done about Ian. He was dead before anyone could get to him. The other one, the boy, was critically ill.

Some minutes before, at a quarter to ten, the amnesty, somewhat delayed by last-minute technicalities, had been broadcast on television before being more widely broadcast by wireless and Fleet Street. The few people in Mallaig who had seen it had tried to tell the crowd but, as they obviously did not have the power of foresight, their attempts were half-hearted. By the time *Rob Roy* slid to the

142

bottom of the dirty, grey harbour about two hundred people at the back of the crowd knew.

Callum was immediately rushed to hospital, first in Oban, then down to Glasgow by helicopter. One doctor described his condition as 'critically unstable'. A second referred to him as 'teetering on the brink'.

Back on the jetty there was dead silence for five minutes. There can be nothing more silent than a stunned crowd. Not a murmur, or a cough, or a whisper broke the spell. Then, as the first police boat reached the jetty and Callum was rushed away whilst someone pulled a sheet over Ian's face, something snapped. They surged forwards, yelling their hate and fury. The police were forced back on to their launch to escape the frenzied mob.

And bad news travels fast. Before the incident could be explained or suppressed, the news had reached Pirate in Oban. They told Glasgow and Edinburgh, who quickly shuttled it on to London. The Secretary of State for Scotland heard it from a stunned Opposition MP who held the constituency beside his own.

His only reaction was, 'Dear God.' There was desolation in the simplicity. No anger, or shame or pain . . . Just 'Dear God.'

The Last Run

Blue Dog left Shetland on Tuesday afternoon, stocked to the hilt for a long stretch at sea, happy in the knowledge that Jim had pulled off a great coup as regards the amnesty. They headed straight out into the North Sea, towards Norway. During the day four RAF Nimrods, the highly-sophisticated reconnaissance aeroplanes Ian had seen on his way to St Kilda, flew within a mile of the boat.

As night came, snowclouds began to build up all along the eastern horizon, huge and fluffy in the orange sunset. Siberia had more winter to throw at Western Europe. It was tiring navigating in an unfamiliar sea, nothing could be taken for granted and there were no landmarks to steer by. Emma took over at dusk, allowing Jim to go downstairs and sleep. She held her course fifty miles west of Norway, until they were beyond Bergen. As she sat, alone, she thought about her position. The rest in Shetland had been much needed. Although she did not want to tell Jim, she had been in considerable pain ever since the shooting. By luck, more than design, her wounds had remained sewn up and were beginning to knit. She would always bear a disfiguring scar or two, but that was a minor problem. The pain, she decided, stemmed from the ragged ends of torn muscles. After the shooting there had been a big bruise, purple-blue, around the wound. She had thought that this was par for the course. But now she was a little worried.

The bruise was as livid and untouchable as it had been a week before. She feared that, whenever she moved suddenly, especially when the moving involved her right arm, the wound would tear open again. This fragility would also explain the constant, dull, nagging pain. She found that she needed more sleep than ever before in her life and sudden movement was a mistake.

However, she also knew that Jim was in great pain a lot of the time. He had fainted on the boat just after leaving Thurso. After the wound in his shoulder had opened when he fell into the sea, he had bled a great deal. He had gone to a doctor in Stromness who helpfully told him to lie up for a week or two. The rest had been good for both of them, but two or three days at sea, together with the constant worries, would get them back on to the downward slide. It was a matter of time before they would both be forced to give up because of weakness, if nothing else.

Emma altered course, cutting back in the direction of Scotland. She was thinking about Jim when she heard a groan from below. She listened, turning her attention to the slight noise. Jim groaned again, saying something indistinct in his sleep. His breathing quickened suddenly and became broken, gasping. She stood up and moved to the head of the stairs, listening.

Suddenly there was a strangled cry. '*Noooooooo.*' It was empty, infinitely sad.

Emma jumped about a foot in the air, then ran down the stairs. Jim was sitting up in bed, his eyes wide open. Black sweat-marks stained his tee-shirt and glistened in beads all over his body.

'What is it, Jim?'

He looked at her and his face was racked with sorrow, tears rolled down his cheeks. 'He's gone.'

'Who?'

'Gone,' he said again emptily. A huge sob heaved his

chest. He collapsed back on to the pillow and was asleep again.

Emma stood over him for five minutes before returning to the cabin. She was shivering all over; although *Blue Dog* was warm, it had been eerie and disconcerting to see Jim in that condition. She lit a cigarette with shaking hands and sat down at the controls, drawing heavily.

When he appeared in the morning, carrying two cups of coffee, Jim was bright and smiling. He was so jovial, in fact, that Emma wondered whether it was she, rather than he, who had been the victim of a weird dream.

'You had a nightmare last night.'

'Really?'

'Yeah, don't you remember it?'

'Nope.'

'You said, "He's gone". It was really scarey.'

'Wonder who I was dreaming about?'

'So did I, I can tell you. You scared the shit out of me.'

'Sorry.'

And so the dream was forgotten.

As the day dragged by they listened bemusedly to the Norwegians radioing each other. The language was amusing, guttural and jerky. It sounded like a joke language. They crossed the North Sea, alone on the big, cold expanse of grey water. They talked very little. Everything had been decided prior to leaving Shetland and there was nothing else to say. They had now been closeted with each other for eleven days and knew each other in a way that friends, even lovers, rarely experience. This was a bond of love, knowledge, respect far more intimate than merely physical. There was nothing that they did not know about each other and they knew without asking, or speaking, when the other was angry, or uptight, or depressed, or in pain. There had to be some kind of telepathy or they would have gone berserk, on a prison in

146

which the furthest possible distance one of them could be from the other was about thirty-five feet.

On the second day after leaving Shetland they were forced to turn and run for shelter as the deceptively pretty snowclouds lumbered across the sea, chasing them westwards. It was becoming rough but they were being driven onwards, rather than backwards or sideways, by the gathering storm.

Even so they were glad to see the lights of Aberdeenshire stretching away southwards, twinkling on the crystal-clear horizon. Jim hugged around the headland of Fraserburgh and sped on along the coast of Banff and Moray. He stopped at last in the sheltered Findhorn Bay twenty-five miles short of Inverness by sea. There they grabbed a few hours' sleep before moving on again at two in the morning. *Blue Dog* passed Nairn and swung around Fort George into the inner Moray Firth. To starboard the Black Isle loomed, bulky and forbidding. Ahead were the new road bridge across the firth and the lights of Inverness. Avoiding the River Ness, which runs through the middle of the town, they went a mile further and entered the first stretch of the Caledonian Canal. After half an hour they were into Strath Dores at the head of Loch Ness.

Jim held on until dawn, determined to put some distance between himself and Inverness. The snowcloud had still not reached them although the first flakes were beginning to fall on the streets of Inverness. Both Emma and Jim deeply mistrusted the wisdom of passing down Loch Ness. There was no escape if they were identified and chased. However, as the only alternative route back to the west coast meant braving Cape Wrath again the argument was purely academic. Jim had come close to contracting frostbite after his dip in the sea on the way to Thurso, and would rather have taken a short cut up the River Styx than go through that again.

All the way up Loch Ness the Grampian Mountains, the Cairngorms, Monadhliaths, Glen Moriston, the highest, cruellest mountains in Scotland, were covered with snow. In places the snow lay on the pebbly beaches of Loch Ness, right to where the water licked and dissolved it. Even the water did not seem to be inviolate. Chunks of ice floated around with impunity, a phenomenon rarely seen on such a large loch.

That night, Friday the first of February, there was snow in the Grampian Highlands of nightmare proportions. All day Emma and Jim had been going through the motions of a very laid-back argument. Due to a certain amount of drug-induced relaxation born of mixing cocaine with morphine, it was conducted with such long interludes between each new comment, that they often had to think for some time before recalling what they had said last. The gist of the debate was that Jim said it would not snow because it was too warm.

Ten minutes later Emma answered, slurring slightly. 'It always snows after the atmosphere warms up a little . . . something . . .' she claimed unsurely, ' . . . to do with cloud cover.'

Some minutes later Jim decided to dispute this. 'Bull. I heard something on the radio which said that that's a total fallacy.'

And so on, all day.

They were drawing near to Fort Augustus when Emma suddenly laughed. It had been at least half an hour and a further half-bottle of whisky each since the last sentence and Jim turned to her, puzzled.

'What's the joke?'

Emma grinned and nodded her head back into the half-light of dusk back up the glen. Jim squinted out of the window. He swore under his breath. For about a mile the glen was perfectly clear. Every detail, every light, plume of

148

smoke, bark of a dog was part of a twilit three-dimensional tableau. Then the view stopped dead. It became a two-dimensional, swirling wall of cloud, advancing closer and closer like a tidal wave. As Jim watched lights dimmed, became hazy and flicked out.

'I win,' Emma said quietly.

'What do I owe you?' The bet had first come into existence around midday. Throughout the afternoon it had grown ridiculously large as they emphasized their arguments.

Emma laughed. She answered, ticking the bets off the fingers of her left hand, 'You owe me . . . let's see. All of your money, your possessions, the lives of most of your relatives . . . um, your own life, as well.'

'Can I write an IOU?'

Emma laughed again. 'Well, as there isn't any of the first, I don't really want the second and I can do without the third . . . And I'd look bloody silly accepting the fourth, so I let you off.'

'Sweet girl,' Jim remarked with a snort of laughter. Emma blew out a series of smoke rings through which Jim absentmindedly stuck his right forefinger as they came to him. She gave him a coy smile.

'I do my best.'

'You do, too,' he answered. He grinned. 'Your last "best" was damned near the death of me.'

'Chauvinist.'

Jim contemplated this for a second with a puzzled frown. Then he looked at her, smiling faintly. 'Why chauvinist?'

'Don't know.'

'I mean, how could I possibly be called a chauvinist? You're the toughest, meanest, most possessive, dominating person I've ever met. You're one of the few people on earth I've ever been scared of.'

'Sorry, I meant cad.'

149

'*Cad?* You're kidding . . . Cad? Jesus. I've been called a shit, a liar, a crook, a moron, an irresponsible little bastard, even a dolt . . . But *cad?*' He walked across to Emma and put his arms around her waist. 'I'm quite proud of myself,' he concluded. He kissed her once on the lips, just a peck, and began to pull away.

'Oh, come on. Geez a brek.'

They kissed again, this time for a long, passionate minute.

During the night Emma awoke, wondering what the hell she was doing awake. The boat was rocking and sighing in a strong but peculiarly silent wind. She could hear Jim breathing close by, and the waves slapping against the side of the boat and the faint whining of the wind in the aerials. But it was that muffled, eerie, mesmerizing sound of the wind talking to itself that kept her awake.

After some minutes Emma shook herself out of the trance which was slowly lulling her back to sleep again, to wonder a second time what she was doing awake. She briefly tried counting sheep but her mind refused to comply. She found herself incapable of painting a mental picture of one sheep. All she got were images of bleak moors, covered in greying heather and patches of dirty, old snow. The wind whispered and muttered in amongst the scrubby heather. Gradually the image formed itself into a dream and she was asleep again.

When they awoke in the morning and stumbled into their clothes, after dawn, the snow was lying six inches deep on the jetty and the boat. It had drifted up against obstacles, blanketing them with down and shutting the grey light from the windows. Jim put on a heavy overcoat and mittens and went outside. He untied the boat and swept the snow from the windows. It was hard work but he finished it as quickly as he could and rushed back to

150

the warmth of the cabin, taking a flying kick at a pile of snow on the deck. His toe hammered into something hard and unyielding. He howled in pain and hopped back to the cabin, tears starting from his eyes. By the time he had removed his shoe and sock the nail on his big toe was black.

Emma eyed it with disgust. 'How d'you do that?'

'Kicked something covered with snow.'

'Wally,' she replied simply.

'Don't I get any sympathy?'

'No.'

'But I'm in pain.'

'Big deal. D'you want me to kiss it better, or what, you great wetty?'

Jim rolled his eyes and let his tongue loll out in mock ecstasy.

'Pervert,' Emma said in disgust.

'All I want is love and affection.'

Emma was about to answer when the radio, which she had turned on for the first time in some days, crackled into life. A distant voice, badly distorted by interference, could be heard. They both instantly knew that it could be for them, as it was the private band used by Radio North-West. Forgetting his toe Jim ran to the set. For a moment he fiddled with the tuner. The voice spoke again, still distorted but much clearer.

'Pirate to *Blue Dog*, Pirate to *Blue Dog*, come in, *Blue Dog*.'

Despite the interference the voice expressed resigned dejection, as if this ritual had been going on for some time with little hope of success. Jim picked up the receiver and answered.

'*Blue Dog* to Pirate, we read you.'

There was a brief silence and then a quick, breathless reply, '*Blue Dog*, is that you?'

151

'It sure isn't the *Tirpitz*,' Jim replied.

There was a loud, relieved sigh. 'Fuck, it's good to hear you again, *Blue Dog*. We were beginning to give up hope.'

'Nice to be wanted,' Jim remarked. Behind him Emma laughed.

'Where in God's name have you been?'

'Oh, around and about. Sorry we didn't hear you earlier, the tuner's been out of whack.'

'Out of what? . . . Oh, forget it. Listen, we all thought they'd got you like . . .' He stopped warily and then continued, choosing his words carefully. ' . . . When was the last time you read the news?'

'A few days ago. Why?'

'When? Be more specific.'

'I don't know – Monday, Tuesday morning. Why? What's happened?'

'Oh Christ,' the man at the far end groaned. There was a long silence.

'What's happened?' Jim asked again. There was something bad going on and they had not heard.

'Look. Listen to the news. It's in a few minutes . . . Oh fuck,' he groaned again.

They listened to the news when it came on. There was a special feature about the amnesty, the police, the government and the accidental killing of Ian MacGillavray as he entered Mallaig harbour to give himself up. Before it was over neither Jim nor Emma was listening any more. They stared blankly at each other for what seemed like an eternity.

'No,' Jim said faintly. He went on, his voice dangerously matter of fact, 'That was my fault.'

Emma fell into his arms, bursting into spasms of sobbing, her body heaving as each new hiccup of anguish shook her. Her tears soaked Jim's chest.

'It's not true,' she cried out, defying Jim, or God, or

152

both to tell her that it was. Neither Jim nor God answered. True to his British public-school upbringing Jim did not weep. He stood, limp with shock . . . and despair. Someone had once told Jim that he was a fool if he thought that grief and sorrow were the same. He had not realized the difference then. Now he knew. Sorrow is acute unhappiness. With sorrow there is, at least, the capacity to mourn. But what Jim now experienced was all-consuming grief which had no words to comfort itself. It was a vacuum of emotion in which nothing else could exist but black emptiness.

While Emma drove the boat, her cheeks glistening with tears, Jim sat, paralysed. Dead to the world he stared blankly at the passing shoreline.

After an hour of this silent, petrified state Emma turned to Jim. 'Cry,' she said simply.

Jim looked confused, lit a cigarette. 'Can't,' he replied pathetically. 'Don't know how to.'

They passed into the northern end of Loch Lochy in the middle of the morning. The snow was letting up, the great, heavy clouds lifting above the mountains.

'Go to Ballachulish,' Jim said quietly. Emma nodded without question. They entered the Caledonian Canal again at Gairlochy, and were soon beyond the snow-covered streets of Fort William and into Loch Linnhe.

At three o'clock in the afternoon they slowly moved through the Corran Narrows and turned to port around the steep shoulder of Benn Na Cucaig, which slides into the cold water up the road from North Ballachulish. They went under the A82 road to Inverness and were in Ballachulish at half-past three. Jim stood up for the first time in hours.

'I'll be back at dusk,' he said without waiting for questions and was off up the road into the town, huddling deep inside his heavy, dun-green greatcoat. He stopped for a

few minutes in a pub and talked to the barman. They
talked for a bit, agreed on something, and five minutes
later Jim was in the driving seat of a Morris Minor. It was
cold and took a long time to start. When the engine
coughed metallically into life Jim coaxed it with the acceler-
ator, slammed it into gear and accelerated through the
town, heading for Glencoe.

Twice before he had come to this dark, terrifying, bleak
valley in times of crisis. The first time had been when his
father had died. Ian had taken him then. It had been a
dark, stormy day in late summer, lightning flickering over
Rannoch and growls of thunder echoing down the glen.
Ian had driven in silence, allowing the full horror of the
place to sink into his young friend. That time Jim had come
out so shaken that he could not speak. But the peculiar trick
had the desired effect. It made his grief tangible by adding
a sort of gothic horror to it. Glencoe, by dint of its impress-
ively unpleasant aura, gave voice to his grief.

The second time had been in the spring. He had been
forced to sell most of the ancestral estate to pay the
crushing death duties his father's demise brought on the
family. Again he had driven, this time alone, to Glencoe.
It had been a beautiful, clear morning. Somehow the glen
was even more awful then. There was a perverse defiance
in the way it stood like the gates of hell in amongst the
pastoral prettiness of spring.

But this time was the most powerful of all. If Ian or Jim
had ever been asked why they went to Glencoe, of all
places, when they were going through appalling personal
crises, they would have been unable to answer. There is
something about Glencoe which leaves little for anything
other than fearful admiration. It is associated with one of
the most brutal, unjustified and infamous deeds committed
in the history of a country weaned on terrible violence. But
it is not that which gives the glen its power. If the forty or

154

so MacDonalds who died had been murdered, instead, near Ayr, or Stirling, it would have been almost forgotten amongst a sea of blood, shed in hundreds of years of vicious feuding by clans from Roxburghshire to Caithness. But it happened in Glencoe.

If ever there is a place where one can feel the old, cruel, pitiless powers of the earth still at work, that place is Glencoe. It would be no less frightening a place if the massacre had never happened. But, when one looks down from the head of Rannoch Moor, down through the precipitous, black walls at the mountains with odd names like the Three Sisters and The Chancellor, it is utterly fitting that the glen has a bad history.

Jim drove up the road, slowing gradually as the volume of snow increased. At last, as the last light of day filtered through the gaps in the mountains, he halted a mile from the top of the pass, unable to go further. He turned off the engine and climbed out of the car, a violent shudder running down his back as the freezing air struck him. He stared down towards a knot of pine trees, towards the place where, almost three hundred years before, in 1692, the Clan MacDonald of Glencoe had been butchered by their guests. Where the flames had licked through their thatched houses in the darkness and the survivors had scaled the sheer sides of Acriach and the southernmost of the Three Sisters, most of them to die of cold in the hills.

Jim did not think of Ian. For the first time since that morning his mind was diverted. He could not concentrate on both things at once so he gave way to the immediate horror of the glen. He stood motionless, his breath hanging in front of him in a small, freezing cloud. He vaguely noticed the pinpricks of headlights as a car tortuously wound up the road. He ignored it. For a moment, a second before it passed, the beams swung over the brow of a hill and fell on him. After the light had gone Jim realized that it was almost pitch dark. He looked at his watch and frowned. The car, having laboriously turned back, was tracing its way down the hill again. It slowed to a halt beside Jim and a voice shook him out of his thoughts. He turned, dully, uninterestedly noticing that it was a panda car.

'Excuse me, sur,' the passenger said. 'But it'll be colder out than you'll be thinking. I don't advise it unless you're having a . . . unless you're doing something important.'

Jim smiled slightly and answered quietly. 'It was important, officer. I was admiring the glen.'

The policeman gave him a quick, shifty look, as if he thought that Jim might just be a nut. Then he replied cordially. 'Aye, it'll be gey scary at this time o' year.'

'It is that,' Jim answered. He turned away towards his car. Luckily night had fallen and he was hunched into his greatcoat, collar up and hands in his deep pockets. But as he turned his profile briefly caught the light inside the police car.

'Haven't I seen you somewhere before? Bin on the telly, or something?'

'You could say that.'

'Got a brother?'

'Yes. Could be him you're thinking about. He's on the telly now and again,' Jim lied.

The policeman frowned for a moment, then shook his head. 'Ony ways, we must be off. Take care o' yersel, though.'

'I will.'

The policeman wound up his window and the car pulled away. Jim watched it go, a faint smile on his face. Then he shrugged, muttering, 'Wait till the poor sod next reads the papers,' and walked back to the Morris.

An hour later he was back on the *Blue Dog*. Emma ran up the jetty and covered his ice-burned face with kisses.

156

'God, I've been worried. Where've you been?'

'Hell, give or take . . . But I'm okay now.'

They walked back to the boat arm in arm, and cast off. Emma took the controls.

'I've been listening to the radio. Scotland sends its condolences.'

Jim snorted. 'Bit late for goodwill.'

'Oh, I don't know,' Emma replied. 'I've thought about things since you went . . . God, I thought you'd gone and done something really silly.'

'Like?'

'Oh, fuck knows . . . Anyway, I came to a few conclusions . . . about Ian and things.' She said Ian's name quickly, nervously. Even so the attempt to smother the word failed to stop Jim from wincing.

' . . . He didn't feel anything, they said. He died a sort of hero where he'd have wanted to die – on *Rob Roy*. He had a great life and his death will make him a legend.'

Jim did not answer for a long time. Then he spoke, very quietly. 'I wasn't grieving for Ian. He's OK now. People never grieve for the dead . . . they do it for themselves.'

There was no way of answering this and Emma knew far better than to try. Jim was right and he was best left to himself, to allow his emotions a breath of life. What Emma lacked in book-wisdom she won back, with interest, in compassion and understanding.

For a long time there was no word spoken. *Blue Dog* moved on down Loch Linnhe. After almost an hour Emma heard a long, wet sniff. Involuntarily she glanced around at Jim. He was staring out into the darkness, his face lined with the salty tracks of tears. His eyes were hazy, brimming over. No other part of his body shared this outlet for his grief. His chest did not heave with sobs, he did not cry out, nor did his face contort with the agony of sorrow. Apart from the tears he was curiously calm. His face

157

betrayed none of the turmoil that churned beneath. Emma, feeling that even she could not share this burden with him, turned back to the controls and continued her task.

About an hour later she started in shock when Jim touched her back. She had slid so far into her thoughts that even a slight touch which interrupted them startled and shocked her. Jim apologized and kissed her.

'You get some sleep now, my love,' he said, his voice slightly hoarse, 'I'll drive.'

'Aren't we stopping for the night?'

Jim shook his head. 'We have to be beyond Oban tonight, or not at all . . . Besides . . . I have to think.' Emma nodded, returned his kiss and retreated downstairs.

Throughout that night, the longest Jim had ever spent, *Blue Dog* slowly began to regain momentum. Oban fled by in the murky darkness, a dim cluster of lights to port. He navigated around Rubha an Ridre and into the Sound of Mull. What had been snow at the top end of Loch Linnhe now fell as a light drizzle, pattering softly. Jim exhaled a breath of dry laughter from his nose.

'Home again,' he muttered.

Downstairs Emma slept in brief, restless bouts. She awoke every few minutes, feeling more tired, each time, than when she had last started, sweating, out of sleep. Her few moments of rest were plagued by a turmoil of conflicting dreams and images, dark and tormenting. When she awoke these pierced her conscious mind, confusing and disturbing her still more. Most of all she saw Jim weeping silently. It had scared her then, to see such a strong-willed, powerful person fighting a losing battle with his emotions. And when she awoke it scared her even more. There was something unnatural, superhuman about the way he had reacted. Something that would remain, fettered inside his heart, as potent as it was unreachable. The last time she awoke an image was imprinted on her mind, like an awful

158

painting, clear and bold. She saw Jim sitting up in bed, his eyes wide open, his face contorted with sorrow, saying 'He's gone.'

Until this moment she had forgotten about it, relegating it to the back of her mind in deference to more important and immediate considerations. But now her subconscious reminded her and it scared and disconcerted her deeply.

That had been the same day that Ian had died, almost four days before they heard of his death.

After that Emma gave up. She was completely exhausted, both physically and psychologically, by her uphill battle with sleep. She left the bunk, damp and clammy with her own sweat, and made two cups of coffee. She took them upstairs and gave one to Jim. He was sitting just as she had left him. But there were signs that he had moved at some point. The slit bag of cocaine lay on the table, a dent in the white dust where he had dug some out of it. Beside it sat a coffee mug, the brown liquid inside stone cold, covered with a film of discoloured milk. And beside Jim's left elbow was a heaped ashtray of cigarette butts, smoked right down to the filter.

'Thanks,' he said when he saw the steaming coffee. 'I didn't know you were up.'

'Couldn't sleep.'

'I didn't even contemplate trying,' he answered quietly. 'It wasn't worth the effort, believe me. I'm bloody knackered.'

Jim snorted almost imperceptibly. 'I'm too drained to be tired,' came his dry, wry answer.

The shock waves following the disaster of Ian's death trembled through Britain, all the way to London. As *Blue Dog* had steamed through the North Sea and the Great Glen, much had been happening. In the following forty-eight hours there was no time for debating, or for planned action, things just happened.

On Wednesday afternoon the Government went through the tortuous, embarrassing ordeal of explaining the inexplicable, denying the blatant and justifying the unjustifiable to a packed house. By an unfortunate quirk of Fate the uproar over the now notorious Camusrory Affair coincided with a leakage at a nuclear processing plant in the Highlands. As a result the Scottish MPs were out in force, the Government front benches were full in sympathy for the Secretary of State for Scotland, and the Opposition benches were full because the Government was out in force. The press and public galleries were crammed to hear the stumbling, appalled speech of the Secretary of State for Scotland. If it had just been the leakage, he could have bluffed his way out of trouble. Who, in the end, really cared if nuclear waste was being pumped into the sea two hundred and fifty miles from anywhere? But a major police mistake was a completely different matter. Due to the peculiar parliamentary quirk of individual ministerial responsiblity the Scottish Secretary's job was on the line. It was a chance no sane-minded Opposition could afford to miss and one which made the Camusrory Affair even more noteworthy.

They crucified him.

A cross-bench group of Scottish Members turned the debate into the martyrdom of a Government minister. There was no explanation, he said, other than the obvious. It had been an accident; a terrible, stupid, disastrous accident, but a perfectly innocent one. It was obvious that he was as horrified as the next man. But that was not enough to satisfy the House.

Everyone, including the Government, knew that it should never have happened. One Liberal Member rubbed salt into the minister's stigmata by suggesting that, perhaps, James MacGregor was guilty of a frighteningly similar accident. The cheers and 'Ra-ras' from every side boded ill for the Scottish Secretary.

The newspapers, too, joined in the fray. On Wednesday morning the tabloids had all gone wild. Nearly all of them deplored and regretted the accident and treated MacGregor as the Robin Hood figure he obviously intended to be. Some of the papers, however, held back for a day, sensing that too many people knew about the whole incident to make it a good scoop. Four or five made some hasty but thorough research and carried banner headlines on Thursday morning. The 'intellectual' non-tabloids, to a man, did this. They expressed not just regret but mortific-ation at the tragedy. One editorial referred to it as 'an eye for an eye', another as 'the law of the jungle'. In Scotland the *Daily Tribune*, living up to its reputation as a tabloid with some nouse, threw its strongest punch on Thursday. Its lead story was headed, with a lack of tact unusual even for that newspaper,

'Murder of the Innocent'. The secondary headline was 'Children of the Mists Continue to Elude Capture' – someone, obviously, had a vague knowledge of Scottish and particularly MacGregor history and had picked up on this, their hereditary name, as a suitably romantic title for the occupants of *Blue Dog*.

Blue Dog not having been near a town except for petrol stops since leaving Yell on Tuesday, this all flew over Jim's and Emma's heads. Now, on a grey, rainy Sunday morning the small crew of *Blue Dog* had far more personal preoccu-pations. Emma saw that, after his night of thought, Jim was in a queer mood. She spent a great deal of time searching for the correct word or phrase to sum up this mood, and it came to her: he was fey. There are a few Scottish words which are absolutely perfect. They hit on

161

things that even the English have failed to categorize and claim for their own. Fey is one of them.

Jim seemed a doomed man: everything that could happen to destroy him had already occurred and all that he had left was an indomitable, defiant spirit. His few words came from miles away and were only just coherent. Every hour his mood changed, moving from despair to cynicism and lastly cold, calculating anger. He would not let himself be beaten, not after all that the police, the world and fate had sprung on him. Now he had the necessary strength to fight to the death, if need be; he had lost nearly everything he had to lose.

During the day news came on the radio that their case was being reviewed. Murder charges were being dropped, or at least diluted to manslaughter. Jim and Emma looked at each other for a while.

'Now's the time to change your mind, if you want to,' he said with the slightest hint of irony, narrowing his eyes and curling one corner of his mouth.

'I could drop you on Rhum,' he added as an afterthought.

Emma stared at him for a moment more, then smiled. 'So you're going on?'

'Sure. Fuck-all else to do.'

'Then I'm staying,' she said resolutely.

Jim sighed deeply. 'This is no time for being stubborn, Emma.'

'It's no time for being foolhardy, either.'

'So you think we should turn ourselves in? Fair enough, turn yourself in then, I'm not stopping you. I may have damn-all to lose, but you've got a lot.'

'However much I've got, it wouldn't be worth losing you . . . And that's what would happen, wouldn't it?' Emma replied.

Jim grinned and shrugged his shoulders. 'What can I

162

say?' He turned back to the controls. ' . . . But I'm changing my tactics now. This worm's about to turn.'

'Is that wise?'

'D'you want off?' Jim retorted with a snort.

'It's wise.'

'Good. Then the motion's carried unanimously.'

After that they ceased to converse. Jim left the controls at teatime and Emma took over with enough cocaine in her veins to keep her going. They were heading nowhere in particular in a general northerly direction. Gone was the time when, fifteen days before, they had been eager to make fools of their pursuers. Now they knew that they were good enough to elude capture until their bodies gave out.

For a long time, as she steered, Emma had the highly disconcerting impression that Jim was staring at her. But whenever she surreptitiously glanced at the reflection in the bridgescreen he was staring at his hands, or had his eyes shut. Once or twice she had the strong feeling that his eyes had moved off her in the same instant as she looked at him. Then, when she turned her attention back to the controls and the sea, the hairs would slowly rise on the nape of her neck as sixth sense told her that he was staring at her again. Not only did she feel that she was being stared at, but stared into. It was weird and not particularly pleasant, as if her innermost thoughts were being violated, as if Jim were deliberately and meticulously sizing her up. For a while she tried concentrating on other things, or wriggling her shoulders both to dispel the feeling and to show that she knew what he was doing.

In the end she became so edgy that she said, without turning a centimetre from her position at the controls, 'Could you stop that, please?'

'Stop what?' he asked innocently.

'Staring at me. It makes me nervous.'

163

'I wasn't exactly staring *at* you. I was staring through you.'

'It's what you might see on the way through that gets me.'

Jim laughed, with the slightest intonation of mockery. 'What have you got to hide?'

'My sex life prior to meeting you, my bank balance . . . all sorts of things.'

'Suit yersel,' Jim remarked. It is a very effective Scottish phrase used when a person either does not believe you or does not agree with you, but won't say it straight out.

Emma stayed at the controls for three more hours. When she gave up at half-past ten Jim was sound asleep, his arms on the table flanking two lines of cocaine. Emma took the customary pound note from her pocket, rolled it up and snorted one of the lines. She stood, note in hand, staring ruminatively at the second line.

'What the hell,' she muttered. 'Drink and make merry . . .' She leant over, taking great care not to touch or breathe on Jim, and inhaled the second line. Before it had time to take effect she hastily chopped up a new pile of the substance into two perfect new lines. She then shook Jim. He awoke immediately, rubbing the sleep from his eyes. Emma reached over and languidly brushed an eyelash from his cheek. Jim smiled and flicked his eyes to the two lines, then to the pound note still in her hand. He slowly swivelled his eyes back to the cocaine and smiled slyly.

'Those aren't mine,' he said.

'What aren't yours?'

'Those lines. Mine are always ragged and wriggly.' In one deft move he reached out and grabbed the pound note from Emma's tightening fingers. She retreated, laughing.

'How come you're so bloody observant?' she asked, still laughing.

He snorted the first line and looked up, white powder

still around the rim of his left nostril. 'I just know when I'm being had.' He grinned and went to work on the last neat pile.

'You'd have taken a third snort if I hadn't noticed?' he said, half inquiring, half accusing.

'Yep!' she replied unabashedly.

Jim smiled. A few minutes later he asked, 'Where the hell are we?'

'Somewhere between Skye and North Uist.'

He scanned the dim horizon. There were high, jagged mountains in the distance to the right. Capped with snow they glinted faintly under the moon. Closer, Skye thrust out towards the West and hills became lower. Healabhal Mhor and Healabhal Bheag, MacLeod's Tables, squatted like prehistoric twins, close by on the right. On the left, far away, on the edge of sight was the long, flat, black line of Uist, Benbecula and Harris.

'They must be the Cuilins,' Jim said pointing to ominous ragged mountains at the Southern end of Skye.

'Must be,' Emma answered.

'It's pretty,' Jim said simply.

'That's the first nice thing you've said in two days,' Emma remarked wryly. From behind she saw a slight shrug twitching Ian's shoulders. A few minutes later he veered *Blue Dog* westwards and cut across the Little Minch towards North Uist.

They anchored and slept for a few hours when they reached Ronay. Then Jim took the controls again at six o'clock and moved up the coast to Lochmaddy. Once he had docked he woke Emma and made breakfast. She noticed that he repeatedly jerked his wrist clear of his sleeve to look at his watch. He wolfed down his toast and gulped a mug of hot coffee in three mouthfuls. Then he was on his feet and dragging on his greatcoat. He lit a cigarette and walked to the cabin door.

165

'I've got to do something. Could you do me a favour and listen to Radio One for a few minutes? There's something I want to hear.'

'Radio One?' Emma sounded incredulous. 'What d'you want to hear on that?'

'Do it,' he ordered, adding 'please' when he realized how dictatorial his order had been. Then he was off and running up the road to the houses a hundred yards away.

For five minutes Emma contemplated not doing as he had asked just to spite him. She could not bear it when he was being secretive. Then she relented. After some trouble she succeeded in finding a blur of mindless drivel that could only have been the station he had asked for. She sat down, allowing the patter to flow over her head. Then came a song which was far too heavy for that time of morning.

Jim must have been wrong about the thing he wanted to hear being on Radio One on a Monday morning, or perhaps he had simply been trying to divert her attention, split her inquiries, while he went to do something totally unconnected. How anyone, especially Jim, could want to listen to the requests of Janet from Huddersfield, or Darren, aged three, from Peckham, totally defeated Emma. But the song ended and there was an unusually long silence. Sensing something abnormal, perhaps an amusing cock-up, she sat down again. The silence was interminable.

At last the voice of the disc jockey came on the air again. He appeared to have been severely knocked out of his stride. His voice was unsure, the seemingly unshakable, unending stream of words had left him.

'Umm . . . we have . . . we've got a surprise for you today, folks. Umm . . .' – a very nervous laugh then he went on – 'Er. I know it's a bit early for the phone-in show but we've got someone unexpected on the line and . . . er, my producer says its OK so . . . umm. Big hand for Jim

166

MacGregor . . . You know, of *Blue Dog*, Children of the Mists fame. You know about *Blue Dog*, don't you, kiddies; all over the papers.' He was obviously not only severely battered out of his normal composure but was also very obviously angry. It was a children's hour, but the producer had apparently been willing to let Jim talk no matter what programme was on. He was big news.

Until that moment it had not occurred to Emma even slightly that Jim's odd request and his leaving the boat in such an agitated hurry had any connection. Her first reaction was utter amazement, then anger, then fascination, all within a few seconds. She sat back in her chair and listened.

'Er, hello . . . Jim?'

'Hello, Mister Sanson,' Jim answered.

'Call me Eddie,' the unfortunate man offered, clinging to something that could bring him back into his own depth. There was a vague snort from Jim's end of the line. For a moment Emma felt pity for Eddie Sanson, overruled by his producer and treated like dirt by Jim. Then Sanson went on, a little desperately.

'Er . . . my producer says you've got something important to tell us all?'

'Yes, I have.' Jim paused. He sounded great on radio, clear and rich. Then:

'Emma and I don't want your amnesty.'

He said it, Emma thought, as if the whole world was on trial and not just a select few people.

'*J'accuse*,' she muttered with a smile.

'How can I trust an amnesty which has already killed my best friend?' Jim continued. 'Ian trusted you and you murdered him for it. We aren't going to make the same mistake.' There was another pause as Jim gathered his breath and a great many people across the country held theirs.

'We've been found guilty without a trial, hunted, chased,

victimized, and generally fu . . . mucked around. I, for one, and I think I speak for Emma too, am not coming in until the real culprits have been arrested.

'Bring in Roy Stevens and his psychotic friends and we'll give ourselves up. Until then we'll fight anyone and everyone who threatens us in any way, to the death if necessary. We haven't got anything left to lose now. Thank you for your time.' He hung up dramatically.

Emma stood up in a daze, and turned off the set. Sometimes, every once in a while, Jim was capable of pulling the most amazing surprises out of the hat, even for Emma who knew him as no one else on earth knew him.

'I don't believe him,' she whispered.

'*I just don't believe him!*' she shouted, laughing out loud.

Five minutes later Jim appeared from the houses, skipping back down the road, a broad grin on his face. He reached the lone jetty and vaulted over the side of the boat. They met on the deck, laughing wildly.

'Brilliant! God, you're clever,' Emma said.

'I know,' he answered, shaking his head as if amazed at his own cleverness.

'How did you know they'd accept the call?'

'Was it worth the risk?' he retorted gaily.

Emma shouted for the explosive feeling of merriment that overwhelmed her.

'Will they believe that bit about Stevens?' she asked, suddenly serious.

'Who cares?'

They kissed for an age in the cold, morning light, then returned to the cabin. As Jim reversed the boat Emma spoke.

'Stevens'll be after us now. He doesn't know how much we know about him. We're dangerous.'

'I know. And his island's only a few hours from here.'

'So's anywhere on the west coast,' she pointed out astutely. 'Where is it?' she added.

'Inner Sound. Called Skelsay . . . Godforsaken place.'

'He'll try to kill us,' Emma said quietly.

'He won't be the first person to try and fail.'

'Nothing like a dead optimist.'

'Pessimists die, not optimists. Optimists just go on hoping.'

'The bastard's got timing, though.' The head of the Drug Squad was talking to the Secretary of State for Scotland in the latter's office in Edinburgh. The minister had just climbed off the shuttle from London and was in no mood for this sort of remark.

'*Timing?*' he roared back. 'Millions of people listen to that man on Monday mornings.' He fell into an awed silence. Still, after four hours of contemplating Jim's ruse, he could not believe how clever it had been. He snapped out of his reverie.

'I want Roy Stevens checked and double checked.' He stopped and swore under his breath, shaking his head.

'No . . . No, forget I said that. Stake out his island. I want you to see that not one ounce of anything he might have stored there gets out.'

'Already done, sir.'

'Good.'

'It would be no trouble to have him pulled in on suss, sir,' the policeman offered.

'On suss?'

'Suspicion!'

'Oh . . .' For the first time in some days the Scottish Secretary smiled. 'No, don't do that. Innocent until proven guilty, as they say. If he *is* guilty . . . then let's see the bastard incriminate himself.'

'And what about MacGregor, sir?' the policeman asked.

The minister frowned away his brief smile. 'I'm not sure. If Stevens is smuggling it'll be hard to get MacGregor on any charge at all . . .' He sighed and passed one hand through his greying hair, noticing for the thousandth time that he was short of hair on top. 'We'll meet that problem in time. Let's deal with the immediate problems now.'

'Fine, sir.'

At midday, on Monday a warning came across the airwaves from Radio North-West.

'I've got a very important piece o' news for *Blue Dog*, if yer listening,' a man said after a song had ended. Subtlety was over now; instead of using the intercom as they had been doing, Pirate now broadcast over the air.

'You've rid yersels o' the fuzz. Now watch out for the baddies 'cos they'll be aifter yer bluid, as they say. Hold yer silence and good luck from us all.'

Jim gave a little war-whoop when he heard the news. Emma was not quite so exhilarated. Although she had not told Jim, and had no intention of doing so, she had suffered a very frightening few minutes in the kitchen. She had bent over to pick up something from the floor and a spasm had passed through her stomach, doubling her up in agony. Paralysed from her neck, down her right side to her pelvis, she had collapsed to the floor, tears of pain breaking from her eyes. For over a minute she knelt, her breath coming in gasps, red-hot bolts of agony shooting up her backbone. That minute was the longest Emma had ever spent. She thought that this was it . . . she would die here, making coffee in the kitchen of *Blue Dog*. The irony gave her strength and forced her to her feet. She stood gripping a cupboard with whitening knuckles and gradually her strength returned. But she was terrified that the next spasm, if it came, would leave her paralysed for good.

'Has it occurred to you that our luck's been unnaturally kind to us?' she asked quietly.

Jim shrugged. 'Up to a point.'

'Let's not give Fate a chance,' she pleaded.

'Who said anything about tempting fate?'

'Me. We should avoid fighting rather than going all-out to find trouble.'

'They won't be expecting us to fight.'

'Scant consolation when your dead.'

'You're becoming obsessive about dying,' he retorted angrily.

'Under the circumstances, who wouldn't be?' she remarked sourly. She brought her hands up to her face and wiped her eyes tiredly, shaking her head as she did so.

'Jim we're not getting any better, you know. I feel fucking awful every minute of every day. My side hurts so much I don't get a wink of sleep, even if I get the chance. I'm knackered, Jim; exhausted, run-down, aching all over, depressed . . . the works. And you don't look much better, you know? We just can't go on doing this for ever. It isn't a game any more; it may've been when it began but it sure as fuck isn't now.'

She stopped and took a deep breath. It had been a long speech for her and now she stood, clenching and unclenching her hands at her sides, tears beginning to form. Jim looked at her and slowly ran his tongue over his dry, cracked lips. She was right and he knew it. He felt terrible, constantly, and he knew that Emma was not exaggerating about her own condition. He knew what he should do, if not for his own sake, then for hers. But there was a block in his mind: dogged defiance, aggravated to obsession by his sense of injustice. The defiance spoke:

'You can still get off if you want to.'

Emma smiled. She picked up a rifle that had been lying, unused, for over two weeks, on the floor of the cabin. It

171

was the same one that Jim had used at Camusrory. She turned it over in her hands.

'Stop playing mind games with me, Jim,' she said calmly.

'All I'm saying is that you can get off now, if you want to,' Jim replied equally calmly.

Emma rounded on him. 'Of course I don't bloody want to. You should bloody well know that, what you're saying is that you want your own way and you don't want me to argue.'

'True enough.'

'Well I have a fucking right to argue, if I think you're being stupid,' she shouted.

'Have I done anything stupid in the last fortnight?'

'That's a ridiculous thing to say, Jim, and you know it. For a start Ian wasn't dead a fortnight ago.'

'Meaning?'

'Meaning that you had no reason to vent your anger on anyone. Suddenly you've become sort of . . . Oh, I don't know . . . vengeful.'

'Sure,' Jim replied quietly. 'But do you honestly think I'd risk my life and yours for vengeance? I know what I'm doing.'

'Do you?'

'Trust me.'

Emma smiled and put down the rifle carefully, with a small sigh.

'Don't I always?'

'No, but for good reasons.' He turned back to the controls. 'That doesn't alter the fact that I have a score to settle which I intend to go through with. It might easily be dangerous so I'm giving you a last chance to get off, if you want to.'

'An ultimatum? I thought we'd dispensed with those.'

'This is my war, not yours. I'd like you to stay, but I'd also like to know that you're safe, so do what you want.'

172

'I want to stay.'

'For what, me or the coke?' Jim asked quietly.

Emma's jaw dropped and a look of unbelieving amazement came on to her face.

'And what the fuck's that supposed to mean?' she demanded, her voice staccato. Jim shrugged. 'It's just that you've been taking an awful lot in the last couple of days.'

'And you've been abstaining?' she retorted derisively. She gazed at him for a moment and then shook her head.

'*I* know when to st . . .' he began to say.

'To stop?' she interrupted scornfully. 'I wonder how many junkies've said that?' They stared at each other for a few seconds and then Emma laughed quickly.

'Listen', she said, 'you deal with your problems and I'll deal with mine. How's that for an idea?'

'So I get us out of this just to find I've got a coke addict on my hands?'

'Just concentrate on getting us out of it, OK?'

'You can get out whenever you want. All you have to do is get off.'

'I'm staying.'

'Last chance.'

'I stay,' she repeated firmly.

That afternoon was a dream come true for CB enthusiasts. The airwaves from Lewis to Arran buzzed with life as a full-scale operation was mounted by west coast fishermen to shield *Blue Dog* from Stevens' men. There were hundreds of bogus sightings, and somewhere amid all of this, hidden amongst six other boats claiming to be *Blue Dog*, Jim headed straight for Skye. Stevens' men, who had come out in force to put an end to MacGregor once and for all, were led in a series of wild-goose chases all around the Western Isles.

Jim himself shook off two inside ninety minutes. The

173

first one tried to chase him as he left the relative safety of Loch Maddy. Jim led him to Ronay, where he lost him by circling the island three times. By the time he slipped away into the Minch his pursuer was far too confused to give chase. The second launch, obviously called up by the first, made the stupid mistake of not keeping an eye out when it homed in on Jim, and was rammed by a trawler. Crippled, the launch limped back towards Uist. The trawler radioed to ask after *Blue Dog*'s wellbeing. Jim said that everything was wonderful and they parted company. As the trawler meandered merrily northwards in the rough direction of Lewis, Jim and Emma heard it commencing its radio game.

'Ah've got a *Blue Dog* on my tail, twenty-two miles east of Mingulay. Could someone geez a hand?'

Fifteen miles west of Dunvegan on Skye another trawler sent out a series of warnings about a cabin cruiser rounding the north of Skye, 'travelling like a scorched cat, ah couldnae catch him', in the captain's own words. Jim did not have the speed or the petrol to outrun a cabin cruiser so he decided to try and outskill it, hoping that whoever was driving it did not know these waters as intimately as he did. Swinging *Blue Dog* north-eastwards, Jim set a course which would dissect the line of the cruiser, who was heading down the Little Minch. *Blue Dog* limped on, deliberately appearing to be in some way damaged. From a mile and a half away the cruiser saw its prey and banked around in a shallow arc, accelerating to a speed that surprised even Jim. It was not a cabin cruiser. It was a yacht with a motor, and it could shift.

Alarmed, Jim ran straight for Waternish Point, the peninsula between Dunvegan Head and Trotternish, the northernmost limb of Skye. The yacht easily made a second change of direction and leapt through the choppy seas. *Blue Dog* reached Waternish Point rounded the headland and

174

made a last desperate sprint for the Ascrib Islands in Loch Snizort. Once, at least four years before, Jim had seen Ian lose a police launch there. He hoped that he would remember how Ian had done it.

In the ten minutes it took to get from Waternish to the Ascribs Jim racked his brains for the secret of how Ian had lost that launch. It had been during the night, much weaving in and out of reefs . . . What was it? There was some secret that he could not recall. Then they were passing Eilean Losal, the nearest of the ragged little group of rocks, where it was becoming dangerously shallow. It came to him.

'Quick, Emma. How deep's his keel?'

'You what?'

'*How deep is his keel?* It's vital.'

Emma picked up the binoculars and looked at the yacht. She shrugged. 'Couldn't say exactly, but it's a high yacht. It'd need a fairly deep keel to hold it upright.'

'Perfect,' Jim muttered.

'Why?'

'I'm about to take a risk.'

They were now nearing the southern end of the islands. The yacht had gained fifty yards in the previous mile. Jim took a look at the last island. Short of it was a series of knife-sharp rocks. Jim hesitated, the rocks now thirty feet away. White waves curled over some, warning anyone stupid enough to go near them of their presence. There seemed to be one space, a flat path which ran through, in a dog's leg, to the far side. The yacht was now only thirty or so yards behind. Men were coming out on deck, shouldering rifles as they appeared from the spacious cabin.

Jim took a deep breath, put all of his weight behind the wheel and swung *Blue Dog* into the narrow channel. Rock scraped against the bottom and sides of the trawler. Jim prayed that he had the correct place and edged on. He came to the dog's leg. A bullet slammed into the cabin. Jim forced himself not to notice and scraped around the corner. The open sea lay in front as the channel opened into a mouth. He shut his eyes and accelerated onwards.

The yacht had turned into the channel before *Blue Dog* had navigated the dog's leg. Bullets spurted off the water and thumped into *Blue Dog*. Some whined off the rocks into the air.

Emma picked up the rifle and loaded it, pulling back the bolt to slam the first shell into the breach. She walked to Jim and tapped him calmly on the shoulder.

'Was this wise, Jim?'

'Yes?' he replied unsurely, 'I think so . . . Ah, yes.'

The yacht had reached the corner in the passage, and unwisely had attempted to take it in one. With a long, grinding crack the rocks drove into its side. Frantically the steersman tried to slam the boat to a halt, jamming it even more inextricably into the tight corner. The rocks drove through the yacht while the surge heeled it over. The men on board slid around, desperately trying to free the lifeboats.

Jim wandered aimlessly out on deck and fired a few random shots into the sea and over their heads to distract them. A few wild shots came back.

The yacht was a goner. It was not even allowed the dignity of sinking. It just lay, like a whale on a beach, run aground to die, out of its element, shamed. Emma watched with a grin of pleasure, Jim with the narrowed eyes of an expert considering his handiwork. The men on board abandoned all attempts to save their boat, or even to retaliate. Two rubber dinghies slid into the water and the crew, throwing aside their guns, leapt clear of the yacht. Driven by the ruinous surge, it ground up and down the rock that had killed it, now almost on its side; within ten minutes it would not be good for plywood. Jim lifted the

176

rifle and squinted through the telescopic sights. Taking a deep breath he pulled the trigger and one of the lifeboats sagged, a deflated piece of rubber, as useless as a ripped balloon. A large wave rocked *Blue Dog* and Jim moved his feet apart, lowering the rifle.

The men on the second dinghy were rowing away in huge, desperate strokes, back towards the far end of the thin corridor. For a moment the yacht came between *Blue Dog* and them. Jim raised the rifle again and moved it along the side of the expensive boat. He reached the stern, waiting for the dinghy to reappear. Then he had a double-take. He swung the rifle back to the stern and a smile crept on to his face.

'You'll never guess what the yacht's called,' he shouted over his shoulder.

There was a brief pause and a laugh. 'Don't tell me; it's the *Argos!*'

'Got it in one.'

'Serves the bastards right.'

A flash of yellow appeared from behind the grinding yacht. As every new wave moved the hulk fifteen feet in one direction, and every trough dragged it back again, hiding behind it was obviously less preferable to risking Jim's marksmanship. The logic was sound, the choice patently unsound. Jim could see the angry, powerless faces looking towards him. He passed from man to man, knowing how easy it would be to knock one of those heads clean off its shoulders. And, in a way, he would be justified. But it did not even merit a second thought. He reached the end of the dinghy. It looked invitingly round, full of air pleading to be freed from its prison. He pulled the trigger. A dent appeared exactly where he had been aiming and the air escaped, capsizing the dinghy and throwing the men into the freezing water.

Jim put down the rifle and cupped his hands around his

mouth: 'You can swim, ye bass-turds.' He walked back into the cabin.

'Turn the other cheek?' Emma commented.

He snorted derisively, answering with an evil grin, 'None of this pussy-footing Christian crap for me. I'm a pagan.'

They headed north, leaving the men behind with the unenviable choice of swimming two miles back to Skye, or waiting on the Ascribs rocks until someone picked them up, or they froze to death. *Blue Dog* chugged away.

There was sound reasoning in heading for the eastern side of Skye. Jim had already risked the obvious by challenging the *Argos*. He now intended to do the same by hiding up for a while . . . on Skelsay. They crossed Loch Snizort and filled up the low tanks at Uig. Then they rounded Skye's northernmost point and headed south-east. The sky was beginning to cloud over. It had been a pleasant spring-like day, but now in the late afternoon the cold arm of winter was flexing its muscles. The sea became choppy, the sky blackened, lowering to within a hundred feet of the sea. Ten minutes after they left Uig it began to drizzle. The wind picked up with its customarily brutal disregard for anything at sea, and the drizzle turned to a blinding, slanting torrent of real, serious February rain.

At about four o'clock Jim realized how rough the sea actually was. In the few minutes it had taken for the storm to blow up he had thought that Emma's fight with the wheel was simply her weakness. A combination of fatigue, poor nourishment, pain, drugs and her inherent disadvantage as a woman had taken a great deal out of her. It was with sudden anxiety that Jim saw how run-down she looked.

If she were to stand before him naked, as she occasionally did when they had the chance to rest properly, he would have seen every detail of what the last sixteen days had done to her. Her ribs stood out, as did her hip bones. The

178

evil, livid bruise still darkened to an unnatural purple the flesh where the bullet had entered and left her body. Her face, by nature fine, with high cheekbones and deep-set, large eyes, had taken on a hollow appearance. Although it was barely noticeable to Jim, who had been with her all the time, there were patches of shadow on her temples, under her eyes and in the hollows of her cheeks. Where there had been tanned, healthy, translucent skin was now a gaunt greyness. Her movements had become increasingly languid, as if her body knew it had to economize.

But there was a strength there that did not just stem from her physical fitness. There was a mental toughness which had not been half as noticeable before the whole perverse adventure had begun. Pain and sorrow and, most of all, the necessity to push herself to the outer limits of endurance, had stoked an inner power that was, in many ways, far more important than her outward durability.

Jim took this in with two or three furtive glances. He had been worrying about her lately and was beginning to pity her as well. She had no part in this interminable, demoralizing rearguard action that he was so stubbornly fighting, apart from the fatal shackles that love imposed. Looking at her, fighting with the wheel, Jim suddenly understood that, for her sake, this game had to end soon.

Then, when he took the wheel and felt the awesome wrenches as the sea tore *Blue Dog* about, he laughed out loud. Having assured Emma that he was not going insane, he smiled to himself. Not only had he underestimated the sea, but he had judged Emma from an extremely fragile glasshouse of his own. He looked at himself against the dark bridgescreen, turning his head this way and that to gain the best reflection in his rain-flecked mirror. He was lean, he looked tired and gaunt, his face hollow below the stubble. And there was something else, something

179

disturbing: he had a look of ferocity, cunning, suspicion and wariness. It was shocking.

The shock was so great, in fact, that he went momentarily limp. Immediately the terrifying current caught the rudder and wrenched the wheel from his hands, and at once it was moving so fast that the wodden spokes had become a blur. *Blue Dog* lurched into a slewing turn, dragged across the face of the storm by the current, showing at least a quarter of the barnacle-studded keel to the full might of the gale. As the first wave hit in a tremendous broadside, Jim frantically grabbed the wheel. The force of the wave nearly capsized the trawler. The cabin ducked under the waves and Emma lost her footing, crashing across the room into the side wall somewhere behind Jim. Water exploded through the makeshift, Perspex window that the kind people of Ullapool had fixed to replace the one shattered in the gunbattle on Loch Nevis. They had not intended it to withstand tons of water.

Jim had made an error that, by rights, he did not deserve to get away with. But he kept his head and hung on for dear life, thrusting all of his weight into turning the rudder straight again. Due to this presence of mind, and to shockingly good luck, *Blue Dog* survived. The next wave hit the exposed aft, bucking it high. The nose dipped deep for a split second before the tail came down into the trough with a sickening whump. By some miracle, although Jim had no time to be jubilant, *Blue Dog* now faced straight into the next wave. It crashed over the top of the boat but the worst was over.

Through the next four waves they hardly moved forwards at all, although the throttle was full out. The boat dealt with the problem not by attempting to ride the mountainous, curling surf but by plunging straight through the middle. Then, when the waves appeared to slacken fcr

180

a moment, Jim hurled *Blue Dog* back around to its original course.

Although this setback was temporary, lasting only a few, frantic minutes, it had two immediate effects. Firstly, the current had dragged the trawler towards Skye, pulling it about two miles in under ten minutes. This was a problem that had to be dealt with immediately, as the cliffs of Rubha Nam Brathairean, at the top end of the Sound of Raasay, are not among the safest places to be under in a hurricane. The second major effect was that Emma and Jim emerged freezing cold, battered and exhausted.

Something that had been buckling badly under the strain finally snapped. Emma's wound had reopened, drenching her back in the blood that had clotted under the skin. Her composure was as badly damaged. She sat on the floor, her head between her knees, and wept uncontrollably.

For Jim there were no tears. All he wanted now was to rest. He fought Blue Dog away from the cliffs and let the gale drive him southwards.

Considering the violence of the storm there were a remarkable number of boats hanging around in the Inner Sound that night. There were police boats, naval launches, a motley selection of trawlers – and the occasional aeroplane too – all milling around the rough vicinity of Skelsay. At the same time that *Blue Dog* was first spotted off the north end of Skye on the radar, Stevens was beginning to make his long-awaited move.

It was greed, something that will never cease making people behave stupidly, which was his downfall. He could have hurled all of his huge store of cocaine over the cliffs into the sea and the only proof that it had ever existed would have been a few stoned prawns. But he wanted to have the best of every world so he sent out a lone trawler, loaded with cocaine, to drop the gold dust under marker

181

buoys. He made the mistake of totally underestimating the amount of people who wanted to see him in prison, thinking that his reputation still stood him in good stead. It was a disastrous error. Before the trawler had dropped the second of its forty buoys four police launches homed in on it. Ten minutes and a hasty confession later Stevens was as good as finished

Meanwhile, three police boats had been dispatched to check out the unidentified trawler which was valiantly battling against the storm. Its random course not only aroused suspicions but also made interception extremely difficult. Apparently conscious of the pursuit, the small boat performed an impossible manoeuvre, turning a full circle across the gale and sliding westwards towards the Skye coast. This totally confused the police, who mistakenly believed that the trawler was being steered either by a raving maniac or a genius. By the time *Blue Dog* had resumed its southward course only one police boat still followed it; the others had gone south-westwards and northwards, unable to do a similar turn.

The trawler swung north off Skelsay, passing before the nose of a naval launch which was by now so confused by conflicting orders and directions that it failed to give chase. Before midnight *Blue Dog*, now conscious of the pursuit, ran into Loch Alsh and through the Kyle of Rhea into the Sound of Sleat. The storm had risen to a crescendo, reducing visibility to under a hundred feet.

For the third time that night Jim changed his mind. He was unnerved by the chase, believing that *Blue Dog* was still being hunted, despite rumours to the contrary. He decided to shelve his latest notion of heading for Mallaig, and took the pursuit into yet another new phase. The police launch, also under a basic misconception – that *Blue Dog* was one of Stevens' boats – opted for chasing.

The two boats raced towards where the Sound of Sleat

opened on to the Inner Hebrides. They sped around the black bulk of the Knoydart peninsula hearing the huge waves crashing against the cliffs to port, and ran on, allowing the currents to guide them around Inverguseran, Airor, An Fhaochay and Sandaig. Jim decided to make a break for Loch Nevis. He swung *Blue Dog* inside the rock of Glas Eilean and headed for the gaping mouth of the loch.

At the last moment the police saw Jim's ruse. They swung after him, struck Glas Eilean head on and began to sink. Before the boat submerged the captain sent out one Mayday and ordered his men to abandon ship.

By boat it was ten miles to Mallaig, the closest lifeboat station. But it might as well have been a hundred; the lifeboat had already gone out to save a sinking trawler and had not yet reappeared. The sea was becoming almost unmanageably vicious, even for a lifeboat. The men in the tiny dinghy were as good as dead. It could barely hold its own against the gale, let alone the murderous currents and gigantic waves. Instead of being driven towards Knoydart they were being dragged out into the Sound of Sleat. In desperation they fired off flares, knowing that unless the trawler they had been chasing moments before turned back, they would not, could not, survive.

The radio, smashed to bits during Jim's mistake two hours before, did not hear the one SOS call. But Emma, looking back over the stern, thought she saw the red glow of a flare, hanging for an instant in the air before disappearing. She waited for a second one. When it came she became worried.

'What's that?' she asked, pointing towards the vague pinpoint of light.

Jim caught the flash just before it dimmed and disappeared.

'Shit. That's a distress signal.'

'We should go back.' Jim did not answer. They were no more than a few hundred feet short of the mouth of Loch Nevis and safety. Rubha Raonuill, its northern headland, was an area of darkness, slightly more impenetrable than the night, away to the left. Jim sighed. They were so close to safety and yet they could not leave men to certain death. He cursed them for being stupid enough to wreck themselves, and cursed himself for indecision.

'Shit,' he repeated at last. 'I can't leave them to drown. It'd be like breaking a Hippocratic oath.'

Thirty yards short of the mouth *Blue Dog* shunned safety once more and swung back into the teeth of the gale. Emma loaded the flare gun and fired it through the broken window. Her arm jarred back as the rocket whooshed out into the darkness. It shot out like a firework, leaving a comet-tail of sparks behind it, and exploded in a shower of green a few hundred yards away.

If it can be said that Jim was both brave and generous to turn back for his foes, it must also be added that he did not display much enthusiasm. One way or another he had been forced to run for over two weeks and he was finally at the furthest limit of his stamina; he was utterly exhausted, physically, psychologically and emotionally. All he wanted was a warm, comfortable bed and the sleep of total oblivion in which no pain, anguish or sickening fatigue could touch him any longer. His dogged defiance caved in; he knew now that he had to face whatever he had been running from and he had to do it soon, before this futile and destructive chase claimed yet more lives.

But for all that there was little urgency or determination in the way he behaved as they retraced their way towards Glas Eilean, in fact his efforts were automatic, almost bored, contrasting vividly with the wildness of the storm. Flare after flare went up from the murky darkness in front,

184

guiding *Blue Dog* to the exact spot where one small dinghy lurched and bucked on the crushing waves.

Emma prepared to tie a rope around her middle, having attached the other end to the stove down in the kitchen.

'What're you doing?' Jim asked.

'Going out to look for survivors.'

'No you aren't', he replied.

Emma looked amazed. 'Why not? It's my turn.' She began to walk to the door.

'If you take one more step I let go of the wheel,' Jim said quietly.

Emma looked at him, her head cocked to one side. She put one foot forward and Jim's left hand came off the wheel. She saw the muscles in his bare right arm flex, quivering with strain as the wheel wrenched.

'What're you doing?' she enquired coolly.

'You're not going out.'

'Why not?'

'Because you're too weak.'

Emma stared at him and laughed. 'You're kidding.'

'*No*.'

His grip on the wheel slackened, one by one his fingers curled open until only his thumb and index finger held the spoke. The tension was now making his arm, shoulder and face shake violently. Emma looked at him, glanced out of the window and then leapt back across the cabin, grabbing the wheel even as he let go.

'God, you're stubborn!' she shouted.

Jim calmly put on a harness, tied the rope to it, put on a lifejacket and an oilskin, and slid out on to the deck. Slowly, unsteadily he edged to the the prow, picking up a lifebelt as he went. The hull of the capsized boat reared among the waves in front, dull and broken amongst the lethal, glittering rocks. Jim pointed a torch at it before a new wave broke over it. He put his hand up, signalling for

Emma to slow down. Rocks scratched the wood of the *Blue Dog* but the vibrations were barely detectable amongst the splintering, grinding noise of the police launch breaking up.

'It's the police,' he yelled over his shoulder.

'What?' Emma's voice came back, buffeted and obscured by the wind.

'It's *a sea-pig*,' he shouted over the gale. Emma grinned. Wordlessly that smile said, 'Oh, the irony of it.'

Even as he stood on the bucking, slippery deck Jim's mind was working furiously. He had not wanted to come back and had only done it out of grudging respect to the code of conduct he had learned from Ian. And now Fate had put him into the position of having to save the very people he considered to be Ian's murderers. It was with the vague, half-formed idea that there was always some reason, however perverse, behind the workings of Fate, that Jim decided to go on and save as many of the drowning policemen as he could. In some peculiar way the act of doing a thing Ian would have done out of principle, regardless of who was in the water, extended *his* mercy from beyond the grave and expiated the guilt both Jim and the police bore for his death.

It had been at least fifteen minutes since the last flare when Jim began to look in earnest for any survivors.

He flicked his torch back and forth, searching for anything that could have been a human form. Then, as he made a final despairing arc across the boat the light caught on something. He made an exaggerated pointing gesture in front and Emma carefully let out the throttle. *Blue Dog* edged up beside the wreckage. Jim silently praised Emma for holding the boat so steady.

He leant over the side, scanning the water for what his mind had told him was a hand. The waves kicked up in his face, causing him to blink away the salt-spray. A

186

moment later he saw the object again. It was a hand, clinging on to a piece of broken wood jammed between two rocks. On further inspection he could see that there was an arm connected to the hand, and a half-submerged body connected to the arm. Jim grabbed a boathook and slid it out until it reached the lifeless form. He prodded it and the man rolled over, his face caught in the spotlight. His eyes registered dull surprise. Jim threw the lifebelt and it slapped into the water.

'Grab the belt,' he shouted. The man stared at it and slowly shook his head.

'Take it. I'm not fucking waiting all night,' Jim ordered angrily. One hand reached out and the fingers curled around the rope that Jim had tied to it.

'Come on. Trust me, for God's sake', Jim yelled. With a supreme effort the man left the safety of his plank and grabbed the rope with both hands. He plunged beneath the water and Jim yanked the rope, dragging him back to the surface. Then, slowly, arm over arm, he hauled in the dead weight. Although he did not realize it, Emma told Jim afterwards that he was yelling obscenities at himself, commanding his arms to try harder, despite their weakness.

His muscles screamed for release, his hands tore and burned as the rope slipped through them, cramp clawed at his shoulders. But gradually he pulled in the body until it was beside the boat. He reached out a free hand.

'Take it,' he shouted. The man stretched out his arm but a wave lurched *Blue Dog* sideways, pulling it away from the outstretched arm.

Jim reached out once more. 'Take my hand,' he ordered again. Their fingers met, tip to tip, and crept into a monkey grip. Immediately the man had a hold he flung out his other hand and caught Jim's wrist in a grip of iron. Jim cursed, nearly pulled over the side, and let go of the rope, catching the man's wrist. Their hands were now crossed, and the half-dead person in the water was not going to let go; either Jim pulled him into the boat or he pulled Jim into the sea. For a second they held, then with a wild heave Jim hauled the man clean out of the water and on to the deck. Both lay in a dead faint. Then Jim shakily stood up, swinging his arms to alleviate the cramp. Despite the cold he was sweating profusely. He dug his toe into the inert form in front of him and it responded by vomiting violently on his foot.

'Ta,' Jim said quietly.

The man looked up and croaked, 'Sorry.'

'Think nothing of it,' Jim replied, lifting him up and sitting him on a coil of heavy rope.

'Thanks,' he said simply.

Jim smiled. 'How many more?'

He looked at Jim blankly.

'How many more are there still out there?'

The man shrugged. 'Alive?'

'No. In all.'

'Eleven.'

Jim swore and glanced at the launch, now a broken rubble of matchwood. Oil was spilling out in a dull, black slick.

' . . . But the lifeboat capsized,' the man went on, shivering violently. ' . . . They're probably a' deid.'

At this moment Emma, who had been doing a stalwart job in keeping the boat steady, yelled from the cabin, 'Got to get clear. It's dangerous.'

Jim nodded. As Emma slowly reversed *Blue Dog* away from the rocks the man pointed over the side.

'Hey!' he warned. There was a yellow lifejacket with a body inside. Once more the lifebelt went over the edge and once more Jim went through the frustrating task of convincing the man to grab hold. Helped by the first survivor – not, admittedly helped very much, although he did his best – the second was saved.

After that Emma veered away and began to circle Glas Eilean at a safe distance. They found the lifeboat upside down, and dragged two more people on board. It took half an hour, in the most appalling conditions, to pick up five more survivors and two dead men. They were not in good condition; and the longer it took to save them, the worse their state. Two were suffering badly from exposure, and were comatose; another had to be given the kiss of life by Jim. And so the laborious process went on until seven men and three bodies in all were found. After that they found nothing more. Hard as they searched not even another trace could be found.

One by one the bedraggled survivors staggered or were carried into the cabin. Four of the worst off were put in the bunks downstairs. Jim and Emma were both exhausted. They kissed tiredly.

'Home?' Emma asked quietly.

'Home!' he answered. Jim set course for Mallaig while Emma made some coffee for the three walking survivors in the cabin. (She had had the foresight to hide the cocaine before anyone had reached the cabin.)

'You must be Jim MacGregor,' one of the policemen said with a smile. Jim found that he was not capable of denying this. There was no regret or surprise that the man knew, just fatigue and overwhelming happiness that it was all over.

'And you must be the police,' he retorted.

The man nodded, his smile broadening. He shook his head. 'Thank you, James MacGregor. You saved eight lives back there, including my ain. I'll remember that.'

'I lost four more,' Jim replied with regret. For a moment they were silent.

Emma returned holding a tray of coffee cups and a

packet of cigarettes. She placed the tray on the table, lit two cigarettes and threw the packet across the table to the policemen.

'Take one,' she offered. Then she walked across to Jim and slipped one of the lit cigarettes into his mouth.

'Ta.'

Emma walked back to the table and sat down. The policeman opposite her lit up and took a deep drag. He was the senior of the survivors – more lines on his sleeve.

'You're no what I expected,' he said to her.

Emma smiled. 'What did you expect?'

He shrugged. 'Russian weightlifter type.'

'Then I'm glad I'm not.' Another brief silence fell.

One of the other policemen shivered and spoke for the first time. His voice was hoarse and cracked.

'Yer fucking strong, though, I couldnae ha' held a trawler steady as you did back there.'

At the controls, Jim snorted.

Emma looked over her shoulder. 'What's so funny, shithead?'

'Did I laugh?' Jim asked innocently.

She thought about this for a moment, frowning and shook her head, returning his snort. 'No, I s'pose you didn't.'

'Why did you come back?' someone asked a little later. Jim and Emma simultaneously shrugged.

When Jim did not appear to be inclined to answer Emma said, 'Seemed like a good idea at the time.'

'You led us on a right wild-goose chase, though,' the senior policeman said admiringly.

'Seemed like a good idea at the time,' Emma repeated with a smile.

'And where'll the coke be, then?' one of them asked.

Emma's smile broadened. 'Flushed in to the deep blue sea,' she replied.

190

And we're supposed tae believe that?' the man said.

Emma shrugged and took a deep drag on her cigarette. 'Ask the prawns,' she drawled.

It took an hour to reach Mallaig. Then, at five minutes to four on Tuesday morning, more than two weeks after the adventure had begun in Mallaig harbour, *Blue Dog* chugged into the same harbour and gave up the chase. There was no one to greet them on the pier, no one to cheer or chant out their names. But they had won. The policemen knew it and so did they. Theirs had not been an ignominious capture, or unnoticed death. They could hold up their heads still.

Before they left the harbour Jim and Emma went to talk to the old witch who was, as always, out on the pier, while the police rang up their comrades and a doctor.

'So. Ye've came hame?' the witch remarked.

'Aye, we've came hame,' Jim replied. The witch looked them up and down for almost a minute before speaking again.

'You'll be looking awful skinny, though,' she said with typically west coast disregard for tenses. 'But you'll still be a gey bonny pair.'

They both smiled. Emma slipped her arm around Jim's waist and he draped his over her shoulders.

'And will ye be getting yersels merrit?'

'We already are.'

'Oh?' She only seemed slightly surprised.

Before they said goodbye to her Jim gave her a package to keep for the moment. She could be trusted to hold it close to her old breasts until they wanted it again.

'It'll no be good fer yez, thon stuff,' she said as she slid three packets of cocaine under her tatty old overcoat.

'What is?' Emma replied quietly.

'Aye. Well there's truth in that.'

Ambulances took away the four men from *Blue Dog*'s

bunks, as well as one of the other survivors, who was suffering from shock. Then the four remaining people walked in silence into the wet, empty streets and headed for the police station.

Dialogues

Bzzz . . . Bzzz . . . The ringing seemed interminable. Then at last the receiver was lifted.

'Hello?'

'Mummy?'

'James?'

'Hello Mummy.'

'Hello James. How are you?'

'OK.'

'You still in prison?'

'No.'

'Why didn't you phone me?'

'They wouldn't let me.'

'Why not?' she sounded indignant.

'I guess they thought that phoning New York was kind of expensive.'

'You could've reversed the charges.'

'It didn't occur to me.'

A brief silence fell as both people thought of something to say. When they did speak they said almost exactly the same thing simultaneously. Jim's mother repeated her question first.

'How's Emma?'

'Fine.'

'Good. She's a good girl.'

'Yes . . . she is . . . How's Sebastian?'

'Well enough . . . We fight constantly . . . but I always win, so the status quo is preserved.'

Jim laughed. Another short silence fell.

'Mummy?'

'Yes.'

'I married Emma.'

'I heard . . . There was a big article in *The Times*. Bas showed it to me when he last got back from London . . .'

'Aren't you going to congratulate me?'

'Why should I? You've been living together for four years. I don't even know why you suddenly did it.'

'We went to a registrar in Orkney. So we wouldn't have to testify against each other if we got caught.'

'That was very foresighted of you.'

'Not really . . . Just common sense.'

Another brief silence. Then she spoke again.

'So, how did the trial go?'

Jim snorted. 'Which one?'

'Yours, of course.'

'It didn't.'

'What d'you mean?'

'It didn't happen. They couldn't find anyone other than us who saw the fight.'

'That was lucky.'

'Yes, it was . . . Besides, they were preoccupied.'

'Oh?'

'Yeah, well the jury would've acquitted us.'

'You seem very sure,' she said.

Jim laughed quickly. 'I *know;* besides, what with Roy Stevens and half of the known criminals north of the Watford Gap coming up for trial, it must've seemed like we weren't too interesting.'

'You've been awfully lucky.'

'Yeah.'

'So what now?'

'God knows.'

'Settle down?'

'Probably.'

'Good. It's about time.'

'Yeah, well.'

Again they were lost for words. People can talk for hours on the telephone when they have nothing to say. But when they have something important to talk about, conversation becomes extremely difficult.

'You must be running up quite a bill.'

'Probably.'

'Well . . . goodbye, James. Send my love to your dear wife.'

James laughed again. 'I will. Send my regards to Sebastian.'

'Not love, yet?'

'OK, send my love.'

'I will.'

'Bye, then.'

'Bye.'

'Oh, Mummy . . .' Jim said quickly. There was a brief silence. ' . . . You still there?'

'Yes.'

'Emma's pregnant.'

'Really? That's great. Sort of war baby?'

'Yeah. You could call it that.'

'That's great,' she repeated. A final momentary silence. 'Bye, then James. Keep out of trouble.'

'I will . . . Bye.'

Click. Jim hung up and smiled to himself. 'Well, that's that over with,' he muttered.

The Secretary of State for Scotland was having his first break in weeks. It had been a bad fortnight . . . a nightmare in fact. But somehow he had emerged unscathed. At last he could relax in the knowledge that enough heads had rolled already. First Stevens had gone, then five leading members of the Strathclyde Police. All, unbeknownst to each other, in Roy Stevens' pay. Yes, it had been a traumatic time.

But the Secretary of State had survived. Today he had attempted to appease the injured parties, as well as the public, with a gesture, tricky but necessary. He had been to see Callum Miller in hospital. The boy would live, although a bullet had permanently damaged his shoulder. Then he had gone to the memorial service, on Mallaig pier, for Ian MacGillavray and had personally unveiled the commemorative plaque on a small cairn at the end of the jetty. And now he was back at his Victorian mansion in Angus, drinking a stiff whisky in his favourite chair and contemplating the peculiar ways of God.

'What was it like?' his daughter Anabel asked from the sofa on the far side of the room. She had been reading a book when he came in but now it was lying across her knees and she was looking at her father. He hesitated before answering.

'Emotional,' he said at last, 'drink, bagpipes and tears.'

'Heavy.' She dragged the word out sympathetically.

'Not really,' he answered. 'It was rather therapeutic, actually. If nothing else, the Scots know how to mourn in style.' He sank back into silence and closed his eyes. After a few minutes he spoke again.

'MacGregor and the girl were there.'

Anabel looked up, raising her eyebrows in interest. 'Oh really? What were they like?'

He thought about this for a while. It was not an easy question to answer. He had sat close to the girl and had been deeply impressed by her general appearance and bearing. She was a peculiar girl, pretty, perhaps very

196

pretty. It was hard to tell. There was a strength, both physical and emotional, that made 'pretty' too soft a word.

'She's odd,' he answered quickly, frowning to remember just what it was about her that had so affected him. ' . . . She's handsome. She's a sort of pretty tomboy. Outwardly you'd call her pretty but there's a sort of look about her . . . an air . . . I don't really know. She's got a look of being what you'd call street wise.'

'And MacGregor?'

'Sorry?'

'The guy, Jim MacGregor!'

'Oh him . . . Yes, he's good-looking. Tough as nails, though.'

'And they're not going to press charges?'

'No, it wasn't worth it.'

'Why not?'

'Oh, Stevens and all that. The powers that be thought that any case against MacGregor would be laughed out of court.'

'I thought that you were the powers that be?'

'At the moment that's a moot point . . . No, I am. That's what I meant.'

'So, in effect, *you* let him off?'

Her father contemplated this for a moment and a wry smile came on to his face.

'I heard something at the service. I can't remember the exact words but the gist was that you'd get about as much joy out of trying Robin Hood. MacGregor banked on that all along.'

'Clever man,' Anabel remarked admiringly.

Her father scrutinized her with distaste. 'You admire him?'

'Don't you?' she retorted.

He shrugged almost imperceptibly. 'He's a junkie, a killer . . . He's the worst combination on earth: clever and

197

wild. People like that are dangerous, destructive. Why should I admire a man like that?'

'Because he's a hero. I bet the Sheriff of Nottingham said the same about Robin Hood . . . I think, perhaps, I could get a crush on a man like that.'

The Secretary of State laughed, closing his eyes again and leaning back in his chair. 'I object to being likened to the Sheriff of Nottingham, but I know what you mean. Heroes are all very well, if you don't happen to be at the receiving end of their heroism.'

'But aren't you a bit glad that he didn't get punished, even if he was in the wrong?'

'Maybe a bit . . . I don't know. I'm just glad that it wasn't my daughter who got in with him. He may be a hero and all that, but you'd have to be tough not to get burned up living in his shadow. Maid Marion must have been a hellish tough gel.'

Anabel laughed, picking up her book again. 'We should invite them to stay.'

Her father opened one eye and looked at her with obvious distaste. 'There,' he said slowly, 'I draw the line.'

Epilogue

It was a calm, still hazy evening in May. Seagulls wheeled and screamed over the cliffs in swirling thousands, glorying in their total freedom, untarnished by human interference. Away to the west the sun was setting, a great scarlet globe hanging above the grey hills of southern Skye. No feature could be made out on Skye, it was a grey outline, silhouetted against the shimmering sky. Southwards, beyond where the battered, precipitous cliffs of Knoydart dropped away to the south-west, the Sound of Sleat, calm as a millpond, opened to reveal the dim shapes of Eigg and Rhum, the Inner Hebrides.

Inland the ground rose, rock-strewn and sparsely covered with purple heather, heat-scorched grass and stunted, gnarled trees. A few sheep, thin and tough, wandered aimlessly on the hill, grazing sporadically. A curlew called, its rising whistle carrying far across the dusty, airless moor. It was answered by the rich rattle and 'Go-back, Go-back' of a roosting grouse. Against the deep sapphire of the darkening eastern sky two people were wandering down towards the cliff. Some of the sheep, suddenly noticing the newcomers, took fright and ran a little way before forgetting what it was that had disturbed them and returning to their timeless pastime of tearing up the coarse grass. Apart from that, Nature ignored this minuscule intrusion by mankind, as if it knew and trusted these two people.

They walked unhurriedly to the brink of the cliff, picking their way down a rough sheep path, arm in arm. When they reached the point where the hill suddenly gave way to the blue-green sea, dropping unexpectedly in a two-hundred foot precipice, they sat down on a smooth boulder. For a while they talked quietly.

'So if it's a boy?' asked the man.

'Ian.'

'Good. You don't mind?'

'Course not.'

They sank into silence, staring out towards Skye, awed by the unfettered beauty. The boy spoke once more, still looking across the sound towards where the sun was now cut in half, dissected by a band of mist.

'And if it's a girl?'

'Pandora?'

'Why Pandora?'

She did not answer for a while. Then she let out a small laugh. 'D'you remember the story?'

'What, about Pandora?'

'Yes; the legend; Pandora's box.'

The man laughed when he realized what she was getting at. 'Yes, that's good. I like that.'

For a few minutes they were both silent before Jim spoke again. 'And the coke? You'll stay off it until the baby's born?'

She nodded wearily. 'I'll stay off it.' She said it as if it were the thousandth time she had been obliged to say the same thing in order to convince Jim.

'If *you* will,' she added.

'I will,' he said. 'Though it's damned near my definition of an utter nightmare to have to sit next to a small wheel-barrow's worth of the stuff for another six months.'

200

'Think *you've* got problems,' Emma replied, she placed a hand on her stomach and grimaced theatrically.

'Tell you one thing, though,' she went on. Jim turned to her, his eyebrows arched questioningly. A slow smile crept onto Emma's lips.

'I know it's irresponsible,' she began.

'Yes?'

'But I'm on for the most almighty blow-out some time in November.'

'Funny,' Jim said, 'I'd been thinking along those lines too.'

'Great minds . . .'

There was a brief silence before Jim spoke again. 'Mebbe we should make a date and do it together.'

'I'm game,' she said. They turned and looked at each other, both of them grinning.

'Shake on it?' he said, extending his hand. They shook hands very solemnly and then collapsed backwards into the heather, hooting with laughter.

A long while later Emma sat up and pointed towards the middle of the thousand milling seabirds in the air.

'Look, a peregrine.'

The falcon was soaring through the seagulls, searching for suitable prey. The sea birds respected this predator enough to part as it swung back to the cliffs. But, having paid it this compliment they closed behind it, not unduly worried by its presence. They knew instinctively that they were too large and too numerous to be threatened by a peregrine at a time of year when smaller, easier prey is abundant. Perhaps, three or four months before, they would have been warier. The falcon, in turn, was not interested in seagulls. It made a few rapid, winnowing wing beats and glided effortlessly over the brink of the cliff.

The two watchers followed it, turning to trace its low flight over the heather. At that moment a golden plover

201

came over the hill like a rocket. It sped past the peregrine and jerked to the left. Close behind it, only a second or two later, a large, blunt-winged hawk whipped by, ignoring the falcon.

Despite the obvious competition the falcon was not willing to miss such sport. With two powerful strokes of its wings it banked and joined in the chase. The hunt continued, the hawk – a goshawk – closing in at ground level. However much the plover turned and dipped it could not get rid of its pursuer, which followed with the split-second precision of a heat-seeking missile.

Neither of them, however, calculated for the third party in the race. The peregrine was climbing for the attack, following every alteration in direction below with perfect ease. The plover made a bid to escape, cutting up the hill in a shallow arc. As it slewed around, turning a right angle, the goshawk closing in for the kill, the peregrine grabbed its chance. Folding its wings it plummeted into a steep, spiralling dive and thumped down on to the plover's back. With a puff of feathers and a tangle of bodies, plover and peregrine hit the ground as the hawk swished overhead.

It turned back, swirling around the peregrine, letting out a shrill 'ca-ca-ca'. The falcon, standing defiantly on its prey, opened its beak and screamed back. Furious, the hawk dived in and attacked the falcon and they both rose into the air, mobbing each other viciously. They dived and swooped, moving away from the dead plover. The hawk had speed and size but the peregrine, smaller and wonder-fully agile, had some breathtaking aerobatics in store. It could change directions, turning a hundred and eighty degrees with one flick of its long wings.

Screeching at each other in their own wild, savage language the two birds chased, turned, dived, dipped and jerked and chased again. As their battle moved gradually further away Jim sprinted up the hillside. Emma saw him bounding across the knee-deep, springy heather until he stopped thirty yards away and looked around, searching for something.

'Right of you,' she called. He followed her instructions and picked up the dead bird. Without hesitating he ran back to the rock and threw the bird down, laughing. A moment later the goshawk, finally victorious, reappeared over the hill, searching for its prey. After a while it gave up dejectedly and flapped away. A minute later the peregrine, still raring for a fight, returned and made an equally thorough search. Like the goshawk it failed to find the plover but, unlike the goshawk, it had no qualms about going one step further. It swooped down and landed, fearless, on a rock less than ten yards from Jim and Emma. It stared at them, unblinking, with its round yellow eyes and, opening its beak, let out a piercing shriek.

'Finders-keepers?' Jim murmured.

Emma smiled. 'You should know better.'

For a while they watched the bird in silence. Not going to be put off, it sat and glared back, the last rays of the dying sun glittering in its eyes.

'I got away with it, though,' he said at last.

'Just.'

Slowly, without making his movements in any way jerky or sudden, Jim picked up the plover and lobbed it to the peregrine. It landed in the heather, one wing sticking up and fluttering faintly in the breeze. Arching its long, elegant wings the fearless peregrine screamed again. Then with one long floating hop it jumped off the rock and on to its prey. With practised skill it plucked away beakfuls of feathers from the breast, tore away a strip of bloody meat, juggled it in its small, sharp beak and finally swallowed the meat whole. Jim and Emma stood up very carefully and backed away. The peregrine lifted its head and watched them go, head slightly cocked to one side, before returning to the feast it had gone through so much trouble to obtain. The two people wandered away up the hill, arm in arm.

'We have changed our ways,' Emma remarked with a small smile.

'What d'you mean?'

'Giving back that plover. There was a time when you just had to so much as smell stolen property and you'd claim it.'

'Hardly,' he replied. 'I've always been a great believer in the deserving getting what they deserve.'

'Sort of having one's coke and keeping it?' she remarked brightly.

Jim groaned. 'Bad pun,' he said with a grimace. Emma laughed.

They wandered on side by side in silence, as the sun behind them finally disappeared into the void beyond the mountains of Skye, plunging them into the blue summer night. After a while Emma frowned and broke the silence, speaking in a quiet ruminative voice:

'An awful lot of people got hurt so that we could have six pounds of white dust. Don't you occasionally wonder if it was worth it . . . I mean, was it necessary?'

They walked on up the slope in the warm, gentle twilight. For a long time neither of them spoke. Emma was just resigning herself to the fact that she would get no answer to her question when Jim suddenly laughed out loud. She turned to him, surprised by the merriness of his laughter. He put his arm around her shoulders and kissed her lightly on the cheek.

'Mebbe,' he replied at last, a hint of a smile flickering across his lips.

' . . . Mebbe no.'

204